Prai

Healing Trauma Th

"*Healing Trauma Through Self-Parenting: The Codependency Connection* captures every essential aspect of recovery from trauma. It's an authoritative and comprehensive step-by-step education and recovery process with a brilliant utilization of the 12 Steps. Patricia O'Gorman and Phil Diaz know this material cold. They are compassionate and dedicated professionals who have been in the trenches with this work for decades and are thoroughly versed in understanding trauma and its treatment. This book is a gift to every codependent and the professionals who treat this problem—the book I've been waiting for without knowing it. It goes to the top of my list for bibliotherapy."

—**Julie D. Bowden, M.S.**, marriage and family counselor, cofounder of NACoA, and coauthor of *Recovery: A Guide for Adult Children of Alcoholics*

"O'Gorman and Diaz bring strong credentials and valuable insights as therapists and innovators in the Adult Children of Alcoholics movement to the immense task of integrating modern trauma theory, issues of codependence, and healing through principles embodied by recovery from addiction."

—**Timmen Cermak, M.D.**, past president of California Society of Addiction Medicine and author of *Marijuana: What's a Parent to Believe?* and *A Time to Heal*

"Patricia O'Gorman and Phil Diaz have created a solid, comprehensive pathway for the military community to understand and follow as it seeks to heal its personnel. Accessible to the layman, it provides thoughtful and inspired steps for growth beyond pain and a chance to regain independence."

—**Col. (Reverend) Eric Olsen**, State Chaplain for New York Department of Military and Naval Affairs

"O'Gorman and Diaz have a clear and gentle way of explaining trauma and codependency to the lay public without sacrificing scientific accuracy. They make the principles of healing trauma and codependency easily accessible to the reader. O'Gorman and Diaz give us a comprehensive and complete companion for self-help and bibliotherapy fans."

—**John Pitselos, Ph.D., C.A.P.**

"If you are feeling comfortable with your recovery, it's time to become uncomfortable again! I thought I had healed the issues of my childhood trauma through forgiveness. In *Healing Trauma Through Self-Parenting*, I find not only how I have been affected and how it has manifested in my actions, but now I know how to resolve the issues once and for all!"

—**Debbie Strand**, executive director of Freedom from Addiction Foundation and host of *Sober in the City*

"The twin sisters of trauma and addiction are perhaps the two most misunderstood and misdiagnosed conditions in the field of mental health. Although many practicing clinicians encounter persons who struggle with codependency, they mislabel this as well and fail to understand the deep interconnections of the codependent relating that they see and the trauma, addiction, and stress hidden underneath. The authors, experienced and wise explorers in this realm, explain the interconnections and map out their implications in deceptively simple language, providing a guidebook for those who are interested in refashioning their actions and perspectives. A helpful resource for clients and mental health professionals, I will make it required reading for my graduate counseling students and recommend it strongly to my acute and chronically ill patients and their families. All caregivers, lay and professional, will benefit from its wisdom."

—**Oliver J. Morgan, Ph.D., LMFT, N.C.C.**, professor and cofounder of Resilience Counseling Associates

"Wonderful, informative, practical! So much information presented in a comprehensive, compassionate, and practical way. Exploring self-parenting and applying the twelve steps of recovery to PTSD as it relates to codependency is *brilliant*."

—**Rev. Mary Croswell**, founder of A Change for the Better Center

"In this inspirational book rich with people's stories, the authors describe trauma and our ways of coping as understandable adaptations instead of personal deficiencies. This allows the reader to feel self-compassion and self-caring while seeing the connection between trauma and codependency. Readers will feel empowered to use this capacity for caring, compassion, and connection as they follow the path full of useful ideas, exercises, and meditations through twelve steps to heal their own trauma and codependency."

—**Thomas Lund, Psy.D.**, coauthor of *Narrative Solutions in Brief Therapy*

"Recovering from psychological trauma can seem horribly lonely because it is such a profoundly personal experience. Patricia O'Gorman and Phil Diaz support you along your healing journey. This dynamic writing duo have teamed up to clear a path to your recovery by writing a practical as well as enlightening book that frees trauma survivors from tired, worn-out behaviors. Invite these authors to enter your internal world and gently guide you toward healthy intimate relationships with others, and more importantly, with yourself."

—**Kathryn Brohl, LMFT**, author of *When Your Child Has Been Molested* and *Working With Traumatized Children*

"This book clearly describes what can happen to traumatized adolescents if they don't receive professional help. It also provides useful strategies and exercises that counselors and therapists can adapt in their work with adolescents. This is a timely resource for those who work with teens who have been traumatized by bullying, child abuse, sex abuse, parental addiction, death, or other traumatizing events and want to break the trajectory of trauma to substance abuse, codependency, or a combination of both."

—**Ellen Morehouse, LCSW, CASAC**, executive director of Student Assistance Services Corporation

"Patricia O'Gorman and Phil Diaz have done a wonderful job of creating an understandable and user-friendly guide to healing emotional and psychological trauma. The reader will surely come out with a clarified and digestible picture of how growing up in a trauma-engendering environment may have affected them along with a sense of what to do with that knowledge that is clear, constructive, and manageable."

—**Tian Dayton Ph.D., T.E.P.**, author of *Emotional Sobriety* and *The ACOA Trauma Syndrome*

HEALING TRAUMA

Through Self-Parenting

The Codependency Connection

By Patricia O'Gorman, Ph.D.,
and Phil Diaz, M.S.W.

Health Communications, Inc.
Deerfield Beach, Florida

www.hcibooks.com

Library of Congress Cataloging-in-Publication Data

O'Gorman, Patricia A.
  Healing trauma through self-parenting / the codependency connection / Patricia O'Gorman
and Phil Diaz.
    p. cm.
  Includes bibliographical references and index.
  ISBN 13: 978-0-7573-1614-2 (paperback)
  ISBN 10: 0-7573-1614-X (paperback)
  ISBN 13: 978-07573-1641-8 (ebook)
  ISBN 10: 0-7573-1641-7 (ebook)
    1. Psychic trauma.   2. Codependency.   3. Self-management (Psychology).   4. Twelve-
step programs.   I. Oliver-Diaz, Philip, 1948–.   I. Title.
  BF175.5.P75046 2012
  617.7'130651—dc23

                                                                    2012002083

HCI, its logos, and marks are trademarks of Health Communications, Inc.

Publisher: Health Communications, Inc.
          3201 S.W. 15th Street
          Deerfield Beach, FL 33442–8190

Cover and interior design by Lawna Patterson Oldfield

From Patricia

To **Kathy** and **Parker**,
Mom and **Dad**

From Phil

To **Molena**,
for all your encouragement,
honesty, and love

CONTENTS

FOREWORD

EDITOR'S NOTE: *Healing Trauma Through Self-Parenting: The Codependency Connection* is intended for anyone who has experienced trauma. While it has a broad-based application, a very specific and emerging need for this modality has been identified in our military population—both those troops who are recently returned from conflicts and those who may have been home for a long time. Because of their sense of immediate need for this text, the authors reached out to a colleague who is well versed in dealing with individuals in military service as well as their dependents who suffer from PTSD and other traumas.

D r. Patricia O'Gorman and Phil Diaz have vast experience in evaluating and successfully treating individuals and groups who have experienced trauma in their lives. In this important new book, they write about how trauma, both psychological and physical, can affect our soldiers and veterans, and how their families and loved ones can be made aware of the signs and symptoms that may arise as a result of these traumatic episodes. A large number of our military and their families have experienced trauma during their deployments and develop signs and symptoms of varying severity. These symptoms may be short-term or longer lasting.

In many instances, the traumatized individual as well as family and loved ones develop codependency as a way of dealing with these issues. To address these issues, authors O'Gorman and Diaz flesh out the benefits of the self-parenting process by including information on trauma, codependency, and the neurobiology of trauma. These self-parenting techniques as well as the affirmations and self-soothing exercises described are not complicated and can be of enormous help in diminishing or completely negating the aftereffects of trauma.

The authors also developed twelve principles of healing, which may be very helpful to professionals and families to soothe the pain of the victim's trauma on a psychological, neurobiological, and spiritual level. These techniques increase the level of resilience for victims of trauma and their families.

As both a physician and a military commander, I recommend this book to all who are involved in the care and the daily lives of those who have been affected by the trauma of war. The techniques described in this book will be helpful to both professional therapists and the families of those whose lives have been altered by traumatic experiences.

—*Robert J. Kasulke, M.D., M.P.A., FACS,*
Major General, U.S. Army Medical Corps

ACKNOWLEDGMENTS

The making of a book draws inspiration and support from many places. First we'd like to thank our editor, Candace Johnson, her design team at HCI Books, and our publisher, Peter Vegso, for believing in this book. Candace, thank you for your solid support, encouragement, and deft ability to keep us on track with grace, firmness, and a sense of humor! This book would not be what it is without your tender attention to detail and your ability to see the big picture each time we changed things. Thank you to our clients, workshop attendees, colleagues, family, and friends, and those contacting us through our website; your courage, stories, and solutions inspired us and helped us to connect the dots about what was really happening in the development of trauma and codependency. And we owe a debt of gratitude to the researchers cited in our book who are seeking to expand our understanding of trauma.

The inspiration for the writing of the actual book came from you, Tom, even though at the time I'm sure that you weren't aware that you were planting this seed. Goes to show you how powerful your thought-provoking comments can be. And thanks to Esalen for creating such a beautiful space that Patricia just had to figure out how to get back.

Patricia would particularly like to thank Rob for being steadfast, encouraging, and loving, and for his late-night and early-morning calls during the intense writing of the book: you really *showed up*. I couldn't have done this without you. Thanks to her children, Jeremy and Michael, for their unqualified belief in her, and for their visits; Ellen and Bill for their wisdom; Julie, Brad, Jane, Elie, Marie, and Judy for getting her through; the students in her research course for their spirited thoughts on the cover during a break one day from class; and Tribal for her head in my lap as I wrote.

Phil would like to acknowledge Paul Alleva and Mike Ross from Lifescape Solutions, Kathryn Brohl, author of *When Your Child Has Been Molested*, and John Connelly, founder of Rapid Trauma Resolution, for their expert guidance in the area of trauma treatment. And thanks to CEO Dr. Pete Harrigan and Clinical Director Dr. Tom Bealy, both of Palm Partners Treatment Center, for their guidance and support.

Phil would particularly like to thank Molena: Thank you for reminding me who I am and believing in me through countless nights of writing and rewriting. Thanks for being my partner in life; this would not have been written without your support and love. And thank you to my Heart Space and Unity Church of Delray family for being my spiritual community and the source of my courage. And finally, thank you to Minnie and Maxie, my dog family, for staying up with me.

INTRODUCTION

Trauma:
The Missing Link

It's never too late to be who you might have been.
—GEORGE ELIOT

Trauma surrounds us. Recent studies show that exposure to traumatic stress is higher than previously understood. Given that trauma exposure is becoming more common—as is awareness about that exposure—it is interesting that most people who have been impacted by trauma do not think of themselves as trauma survivors. For example, serious illness in oneself or one's child; losing a job or a home; losing a spouse to death or divorce; working in an ER as a nurse; or volunteering to do recovery work after a natural disaster—all these can be traumatic. So, too, is the impact of deployment on our military men and women and their families. Because many trauma survivors don't identify themselves as traumatized, they are "invisible."

There is one exception to this tendency not to identify as being traumatized. Survivors of pervasive or complex trauma (see Chapter 1 for more about complex and other traumas) more easily label themselves as trauma survivors. Such survivors, including adult children of alcoholics and children of other types of challenging families, have suffered a more subtle kind of trauma that left them wounded and searching for wholeness. They seek therapy, read books, attend conferences, and go to Al-Anon meetings—all in an attempt to right something that they experienced. Once they appreciate their own trauma histories and their resilience, they begin to address the way that their trauma manifested for them—the only way—the one thing that really caught their attention: their need to care for others. This is codependency—a type of attachment to others where there is a tendency not to take care of oneself while simultaneously seeing to what everyone else needs. (See Chapter 3 for a full discussion of codependency.)

Research—as well as anecdotal evidence from our patients, conference attendees, and readers—shows that what lies at the base of the struggle with codependency—that is, why people cannot take active care of themselves and why the needs of others feel more imperative than their own—*is a response to trauma*. Whether this trauma occurred early in childhood or is more recent doesn't matter. Trauma is indeed proving to be the missing link in the codependency field.

For an adult, trauma is defined as exposure to a one-time event, numerous exposures to horrific events, or ongoing exposure to events such as war or domestic violence that profoundly and negatively affect the person. For children, ongoing neglect or abuse, as well as exposure to a one-time or ongoing horrific event(s), constitute traumatic exposure. Recently, research has expanded our understanding of the impact of trauma to possibly include those who live with someone who has been traumatized, such as family members of veterans who themselves are experiencing signs of trauma. Long neglected and misunderstood by healthcare professionals and survivors alike, trauma is now being seen as a driver of behavior by both the treatment community and those who have experienced its destructive force—a driver that we need to comprehend more fully.

We humans are complex and multifaceted. Many of us know trauma intimately. Trauma and the resulting codependency (with their many faces and numerous presentations) serve to underscore our need to take care of ourselves and the price we pay when we do not. The good news is that finally trauma and codependency are beginning to command the attention they deserve—and so are effective strategies for managing them, like self-parenting!

Self-parenting is about guiding yourself through a process that allows you to become who you would like to be—who you were meant to be—by healing yourself through caring for yourself. How well we learn to self-parent determines how well we go through life.

Trauma researchers have recently proclaimed the need for those impacted by trauma to become the parent to themselves that they needed growing up (Fogash and Copeley 2008). We in the codependency community have known for years that this self-parenting is possible and that it works very well!

Healing Trauma Through Self-Parenting—The Codependency Connection is the first book written for those who have developed codependency as a coping skill after experiencing trauma. It is a survivor's book—or as we say with our strength-based focus, a *thriver's* book—providing a personal focus for those affected. It is invaluable to those who are looking for a resource to help them heal, and it's a useful tool for professionals as a needed and valuable resource in their work with their clients. It complements the growing literature on both trauma and codependency by offering a simple process that readers can employ to begin their healing: the process of self-parenting. We will take you through this transformative process of becoming the parent that you have always needed, a process we have specifically tailored for those healing from trauma and its subsequent codependency.

We will teach you how to parent yourself by identifying and helping you soothe the pain of your trauma on psychological, neurobiological, and spiritual levels. We will assist you in identifying, owning, and growing your hard-won resilience, and we will guide you in charting your recovery as you begin to celebrate who you are today, not just what you can do for others. We will help you accomplish all these things through the use of the self-parenting techniques, affirmations, and self-soothing exercises described in Part Two of this book. The self-parenting process is complemented by information on trauma, codependency, the neurobiology of trauma, the twelve principles of healing, and other sources of support that are available.

This book is our gift to you—and to those of you who have worked with us, shared your stories, and made us aware of the connection between trauma and codependency. We hope the process of self-parenting as it relates to trauma and codependency will be meaningful to you on a deep and healing level, and we invite you to share your thoughts with us at www.ogormandiaz.com. For more information on Patricia's clinical work contact her at www.patriciaogorman.com.

And now, as we say at the end of each step, "Let the healing begin."

Part One:

Understanding Trauma and the Codependency Connection

In the first part of this book, we drew upon the connections between the development of trauma and one of the elaborate—even elegant—defenses developed to function and control trauma's effects: codependency. By examining the latest research findings and sharing the transcendent stories of other codependent trauma survivors, you will learn about the many types of trauma we can experience and their effects in the brain, body, mind, and spirit. You will learn about physical and emotional triggers that can bring back memories of trauma and how to begin to manage them. You will come to understand why codependency develops and, most important, how it can be transformed into its more healthy counterpart—*resiliency*. Get ready to rethink what you thought you knew and confirm what you may have long suspected about trauma and codependency.

CHAPTER 1

∾

Identifying Trauma

*I try to take one day at a time, but sometimes
several days attack me at once.*

—ASHLEIGH BRILLIANT

Trauma is a response that develops when one feels one's life is being threatened or when one has witnessed serious injury or destruction (American Psychiatric Association [APA] 1994). Trauma also develops from multiple incidences of abuse and neglect during childhood and adolescence (van der Kolk 2003). Trauma may be experienced also through living with someone who carries a trauma diagnosis (Yehuda, Halligan, and Grossman 2001). And trauma's impact intensifies when multiple sources of trauma are experienced in childhood, adolescence, and then in adulthood.

Whatever the origin of our traumatic responses, they do not come out of the blue. In adults, exposure to trauma produces an immediate response to the stimulus, whether that stimulus is an event in the present, a triggered memory, or both. We feel this response in our bodies: increased pulse rate, tightness in the chest, shortness of breath, constricted vision, shaking, sweating, an extreme startle response, and perhaps a desire to run or lash out. We may begin to think about the event or memory and try to make sense of it, sometimes obsessively, maybe with racing thoughts. Trauma can be experienced by family members whose loved one has been profoundly altered by his or her experience in combat; by helpers who witness the pain of those they help (the classroom teacher, counselor, or the rescue volunteer); and by generations of peoples who have been oppressed.

Trauma's impact in children is much more complicated; its causes are more varied and depend on the child's or adolescent's ability to understand what is happening. Most traumas experienced by children are at the hands of a caregiver on whom the child depends: a parent; a parental substitute such as a parent's partner; a babysitter; a sibling; a neighbor; or a relative. Trauma in young children can produce confusion, fear, and deep feelings of rage. At the same time that the child is being hurt, he longs for and needs the caregiver to take care of him, to soothe him, even if it is the caregiver who is hurting him. And to complicate things further, depending upon the age of the child, the trauma may not be stored as an actual memory in the brain but in the body as a sensation—a "body memory" (van der Kolk 2003).

For adolescents, trauma may also be experienced as a result of being a friend to someone who is in serious emotional difficulty, or at the hands of peers, older adolescents, or even adults who prey on vulnerable adolescents. We see this in situations where adolescents feel responsible for a friend who has committed suicide; in adolescents who are bullied; in others who are so overwhelmed by school that they find themselves failing even though they are bright; in those who are lured into running away from home and into prostitution; or in those who are introduced to drugs and find themselves running drugs for those who they felt were their friends. There are numerous ways that trauma can be experienced that are unique to adolescents.

Trauma is an unconscious, whole-body experience. It involves the involuntary autonomic nervous system of the body, parts of the brain, and the memory. Seen in this way, trauma is a mind and body phenomenon experienced on both a psychological and physiological level.

Trauma: Big "T" and Little "t"

We often think of trauma as having a capital "T": the trauma of a near-death experience in a serious car accident; the death of a parent, friend, or sibling; the deaths of the family members and first responders on 9/11; the trauma of those returning from war; or of hostages, concentration camp survivors, survivors of religious cults, and survivors of natural disaster such as hurricanes, floods, tornadoes, or fires.

But there is also trauma of the smaller "t" variety—and it is just as powerful: the trauma experienced by a child or adolescent (and felt as an adult) through the distancing of narcissistic caregivers who were more involved in their own lives than in their children's. This distancing might have been the repeated abandonments that a child of an alcoholic felt as her parent left nightly to go to a bar—or whose parent never came home from a bar. Or the trauma could have been from physical abuse, sexual abuse, or neglect; the divorce of one's parents; being bullied by peers as a child, in the workplace as an adult, or as a woman in the military. And there are other dimensions to trauma. For example, there is the trauma experienced by an adolescent whose friend is cutting herself or is suicidal. The levels and depths of trauma that we each experience are varied, but the results of trauma are not.

Types of Trauma

Trauma can be broken down into many categories, and where there is a history of trauma, each category can present a challenge for the individual to cope with. Each current trauma has the potential to pull previously experienced traumas—such as those from childhood and adolescence—back into consciousness and essentially retraumatize the individual. We call this being triggered, something we will explore shortly.

The diagnoses of trauma can be tricky as well. Many times, the symptoms of trauma can look like another mental health diagnosis or may manifest in illnesses that do not seem to have an obvious origin (Maté 2003). To complicate diagnosis further, many in the trauma field feel that the current diagnoses of trauma are inadequate. They have developed other ways of looking at trauma by focusing on the duration and source of the trauma and not just the symptoms experienced because of the traumatic event.

Let's take a closer look at each way that trauma is commonly understood. According to the *Diagnostic and Statistical Manual of Mental Disorders, DSM-IV* (APA 1994), there are two types of trauma that carry an actual mental health diagnosis—acute stress disorder and post-traumatic stress disorder (PTSD). The names of these traumas correlate to the symptoms developed by the person experiencing them as well as to the length of time that these symptoms have been experienced. Acute stress disorder occurs shortly after experiencing a traumatic event and lasts up to four weeks after the event, and PTSD is the experience of trauma once it envelops the person as symptoms are persistently re-experienced. But it is important to note that PTSD may not occur immediately. Symptoms can occur six months or longer after the stressor. Additionally, there are traumas not currently diagnosed in the *DSM-IV*, such as complex trauma—the repeated violation of a child or adolescent by a caregiver. The child or adolescent with complex trauma experiences problems in attention, behavior, mood regulation, and bonding. These symptoms are often captured under the diagnosis of depression, attention deficit hyperactivity disorder (ADHD), reactive attachment disorder, conduct disorder, or even bipolar disorder—without the underlying causation of trauma being addressed (Roth et al. 1997; van der Kolk 2003).

Acute Stress Disorder: Feeling the Earth Crumble Beneath Your Feet

Mark is a graduate student working in a summer-school program. One day, he was walking his dog near a playground when he heard screaming and saw a group of kids gathering around something. When he went to investigate, he saw one of his students on the ground, bleeding. What happened next is a blur to Mark: He remembers watching someone apply pressure to the boy's wound while he took out his cell phone and called 911. He remembers the ambulance coming and pronouncing his student dead. He remembers beginning to cry.

That night, Mark couldn't stop crying, he couldn't eat or sleep, and he felt basically numb. He kept remembering seeing the sight of his student lying dead. He felt as if he was in a daze. He berated himself for not being able to stop this horrific event, though he wasn't sure what he should have done. He felt totally helpless. The next day he went to school and couldn't stop thinking about what he had seen. He couldn't stop talking about it either. Tears kept welling up in his eyes. He remembers thinking that other people knew the student but somehow they could function. Finally, on the second day, Mark was sent home and advised to see a mental health professional immediately.

Mark called a psychologist who gave him an emergency same-day appointment when she heard what was going on. She knew that a timely intervention was of the essence when someone had experienced an event this upsetting. The psychologist did several important things when she met with Mark. She normalized his feelings, telling him what he was experiencing was to be expected when one has witnessed a tragedy as he did. She taught him some self-soothing techniques to control his thinking and to calm himself. Mark's diagnosis was acute stress disorder.

Acute stress disorder is a normal response to a horrific event. By seeking immediate help, Mark was able to control his response, allowing his healing to begin by resolving his reactions to this tragedy. Acute stress disorder usually occurs within two days of the traumatic event and lasts for a maximum of four weeks. If it lasts longer, then a different diagnosis of post-traumatic stress disorder is warranted.

Post-Traumatic Stress Disorder:
Helplessness and Repeated Victimization

Post-traumatic stress disorder is the repeated re-experiencing of a traumatic event through intrusive recollections of the event. Flashbacks, dreams, or intense physical or psychological distress due to real or symbolic cues representing the event are common.

These symptoms can produce problems in daily functioning such as disruptions in sleeping and concentrating, and significant disruption in relationships, employment, and other important areas of life (APA 1994).

PTSD is finally receiving recognition due in large part to our returning military. While not restricted to those who have had military experience, we are coming to understand that PTSD is a common reaction to the strain of deployment and the uncertainty of battle. And through understanding the mechanics of the development of PTSD in those in combat, we are coming to know how PTSD develops in other populations, such as family members of veterans who suffer from PTSD, first responders, and other types of helpers.

For example, when Tessa's husband came back from his first deployment to Iraq, she didn't understand the reactions she had: "I was so tense all the time. I didn't know what was wrong with me. I felt like such a failure. And all I wanted to do was to be a good and supportive wife to George. Instead, I was the basket case, even though he's the one who got the diagnosis of PTSD. It wasn't just his nightmares or his drinking, or that he'd get angry and lose it; I was flipping out, too, and I didn't understand why. I realized that I needed help as well." Tessa realized that George's behavior was impacting her negatively—that he was traumatizing her—and so she sought help.

As we begin to understand PTSD and look for it, we are finding it to be much more pervasive than previously thought. One cause of potential PTSD in the general population is the negative affect on students of the increasing violence in schools and their surrounding community. Another potential cause of PTSD in both men and women is sexual assault or attack with a weapon (*Encyclopedia of Mental Disorders* 2011). Some of the hallmarks of PTSD are fear, insomnia, a pervasive sense of helplessness, and putting oneself in situations where repeated victimizations may occur, such as not protecting oneself at work from the bullying of a supervisor or coworker, or not having helpful boundaries with the excessive demands of family or friends. We may allow ourselves to be victimized by others in subtle or obvious ways. And our sense of helplessness can be general or fixated on just intimate relationships, which in turn can become sources of intense jealousy.

Let's look at Mark again, but this time, we'll assume that he doesn't have an immediate mental health intervention after he witnesses a violent murder at a playground near where he works. The trauma may begin to take hold within him. He may experience recurrent, intrusive, and upsetting thoughts, but might not link those thoughts to the event. He may begin having vivid nightmares, but not realize that he is actually re-experiencing the event. He may act as he did when the event initially occurred, with intense panic or feelings of helplessness but not know why. He may keep thinking about his dead student. Over time, the actual memory of the student's death may fade, and Mark may just experience feelings of helplessness and the body sensations he felt at the time of the original event.

As a result, Mark may begin to avoid activities like walking his dog—without understanding why. He may find himself keeping away from certain topics of discussion. While he may have enjoyed certain types of entertainment before the incident (for example, books or movies involving shootings), now he may find himself either avoiding these activities or becoming very angry or agitated when he is exposed to them. Eventually, he may distance himself from those he was close to, becoming angry, watchful, or anxious and not knowing why. He may also lose his confidence in his career choice and second-guess himself at every turn.

Mark may be triggered into these feelings by stimuli he associates with the original event, even without consciously attaching those feelings to the event any longer. Those strong feelings become attached to something else instead, something more immediate, something he hopes he can influence. He may begin to feel that he cannot trust his girlfriend to be faithful to him and become jealous and possessive, feeling he needs to make sure, on some deep level, that she will not betray him. He clings to her, placing his feelings of self-worth on her shoulders as he simultaneously resents his new neediness. In this way, he displaces his anxiety on to her.

Mark has now developed post-traumatic stress disorder (PTSD). He has internalized the trauma he witnessed and is in considerable distress. This calls for more intense treatment that usually continues over a prolonged period of time.

Complex Trauma: Repeated and Sustained Pain in Childhood

Complex trauma is the term used to describe the impact of child abuse and neglect on the children themselves (Roth et al. 1997; van der Kolk 2003). The term captures the results of repeated abuse (such as directly experienced neglect and physical and sexual abuse of a young child) by a caregiver or a member of the child's or adolescent's family, including older siblings and extended family. It also can be used to describe the impact of witnessing the abuse of another, such as in incidents of domestic violence or the extreme punishment of a sibling (Pelcovitz et al. 1997). The symptoms of complex trauma vary, but the important point here is that this is *sustained* trauma, not one-time trauma, and it begins early in life (Roth et al. 1997).

When the symptoms of complex trauma are experienced in adulthood, some professionals call it complex post-traumatic stress disorder or C-PTSD (Herman 1992a, 1992b). The results of complex trauma can also be seen in adolescents and adults who experience problems in mood regulation, concentration, and intimate relationships, and/or continue to put themselves in high-risk situations where there is a likely potential for them to be harmed or victimized.

Keeping Mark as our example, let's give him a challenging childhood.

Mark's parents' marriage ended when Mark was two, just before the birth of his sister. This resulted in a period of both emotional and financial instability for Mark, his mother, and his sister, but he always felt his mother's love. Mark remembers the constant moves, sleeping on family members' sofas, never having a room of his own, and his mother crying as she tried to figure out how to support her children.

His mother wasn't a quitter. She didn't give up; she dated and eventually met someone she considered very special. They met in church, and she felt that this man had the same family values she did. He was also a professional man with a steady income, and he seemed devoted to her children.

Mark was only seven when they married, but he soon realized how different their lives were. They now had one apartment they lived in, a really nice one, and they no longer had to move from one family member to another. His mother went to school, which had been her lifelong dream, and she obtained a nursing degree. She was happy, and so was his sister. And so was Mark, until his mother obtained a position as a nurse in the hospital working the evening shift.

Life required some adjustments with his mother no longer being home at night. His stepfather was now in charge of the evening bedtime ritual. By this time, Mark was a preteen, and things began to change. His stepfather put him to bed telling him how special he was. Over time, he began touching Mark and then sexually abusing him. At first, curious and liking the attention, Mark complied, but eventually he resisted. This caused his stepfather to become violent with him and threaten him, his mother, and his sister. Mark remembers his stepfather placing a gun to his head at one point, telling him he'd make Mark watch as he killed Mark's mother and sister.

Mark got the message. He was quiet during the abuse. But his grades dropped in school, and he began to fight with his peers. After one fight at school, where the police were called due to the extensive injuries he caused his friend, everything came out.

A kind teacher asked Mark about what was happening, suggesting that he wasn't acting like the sweet young man she remembered. A trained policeman picked up on the question and asked Mark what seemed like an improbable question: was he was being abused? Mark reluctantly answered yes.

Mark's stepfather was called to the school as the "guardian of record." After his abuse was revealed he was arrested, tried, and convicted of the sexual abuse of a child.

Mark's trauma was pervasive. He internalized the negative messages from his abuse, and they became part of how he saw himself—as somehow damaged. He began to demonstrate problems in mood and behavior regulation that children with complex trauma typically experience. With the acknowledgment and punishment of Mark's abuser he was able to begin to heal. But he still had a great deal of anger. Thanks to a supportive school he was able to channel his anger into sports, becoming a star football player in high school, and going to college on a football scholarship. And the support of the school personnel shaped his career decision, helping him become a teacher specializing in working with the type of challenging youth that he once was.

Let's take a look at someone whose abuser was not acknowledged, and how that led to her feeling that she was essentially unworthy.

Amy was sexually abused by her mother's favorite brother, the person on whom the family relied to help keep them together when Amy's father died. The abuse began when she was about three and continued until she reached puberty.

Amy was about thirteen when she found her first boyfriend, who was older than Amy—seventeen, to be exact. He was an unemployed high-school dropout, and Amy and her mother argued about him constantly. In one argument, when her mother yelled at her that she should have more self-respect, Amy scoffed and said, "Like you care."

"I do care," her mother countered.

"Then why did you always leave me with Uncle Chuck?" Amy replied. "Do you know what he did to me?"

"He didn't do anything to you," her mother responded angrily. "Stop the lying! And don't try to change the subject."

Although she tried several times to tell her mother about the abuse, Amy could not persuade her mother that her uncle was anything but honorable. Amy felt more and more helpless because her mother didn't believe her. She sought comfort from other sources. She learned to settle for men who made her feel loved, even if it didn't look that way to others, and she learned to numb her pain with alcohol.

By the time Amy went to college, she had a reputation as a party girl. "I guess I stopped caring about what others thought. I just wanted to have fun," she said. By her late twenties, she'd had a couple of long-term affairs with married men and a major alcohol problem that was creating work issues.

Amy went to therapy and was confronted about how she treated herself. She surprised herself by crying. "Where did this come from?" she asked as she briskly wiped away her tears. "I didn't know this was in there. This pain . . . I guess I never thought I deserved more. I'm such a mess. But I want more. I really want someone to love me, and just me."

Because of the number of victimizations Amy experienced, the anger that she turned against herself had become normal for her. As a result, she also had problems in controlling her mood, and she sought high-risk, sensational activities, almost as if she was punishing herself. She put herself in a position of some control by having long-term affairs with married men, which she realized was essentially an empty way to live. She was surprised to discover that one of the reasons she was such a heavy drinker was because she was trying to numb the emptiness caused by the trauma of the abuse she experienced as well as the trauma of her father's death.

Both Mark and Amy felt "less than." Of course, this is not a full or an accurate representation of who they are. They are actually pretty resilient—but more about that later.

Historical or Intergenerational Trauma

For many of us, trauma is multigenerational. The trauma did not happen to us, but it happened to our mothers, fathers, grandfathers, and great-grandfathers. We learned of it through family stories that profoundly upset us; the stories shaped us and perhaps even traumatized us. This is particularly true for Native Americans, children of Holocaust survivors, and children of adult children of alcoholics

(ACOAs), all of whom have well-documented intergenerational trauma (also called historical trauma), where the transmission of trauma as memory, and sometimes identity, is carried through as a family or a cultural identity. When shared, this information has a powerful effect on those who hear it. In a family, the result can be a child trying to protect a parent who had such a difficult childhood. In a culture, the result can involve feelings of anger toward another group without the direct experience of the cause for this anger.

Historical or intergenerational trauma has been defined as the "cumulative emotional and psychological wounding across generations, including one's own life span" (Yellow Horse Brave Heart 2005). Here, the multiple traumas of one's lifetime are compounded by traumas in previous generations. In this way, trauma becomes woven into the identity of a family or a cultural, racial, or ethnic group.

An important step forward in articulating this type of trauma is the development of constructs that guide our understanding of how this intergenerational mechanism works. An example of such a construct is one that explores the development of post-traumatic slave syndrome (PTSS). Slavery was predicated on the belief that African Americans were inherently inferior to whites. Once slavery was abolished, this belief was followed by institutionalized racism, which continued to perpetuate the idea of inferiority and resulted in injury to those of African-American descent, profoundly affecting all the generations born subsequent to the end of slavery in the United States (DeGruy 2011).

Research is just beginning to focus on how trauma is transmitted. One study of children of survivors of the Nazi Holocaust found "that early developmental experiences constitute important risk factors for PTSD" as trauma was transferred from parent to child. They also noted the high degree of the stress hormone present in parents, and noted how this influenced the parenting style (Yehuda, Halligan, and Grossman 2001). This research and other such studies are helping us to understand the mechanisms of just how trauma is passed from parent to child, an issue of particular concern as more military personnel who have children are returning from deployment suffering from PTSD.

Secondary Trauma: Compassion Fatigue

Secondary or vicarious trauma, also called compassion fatigue, is not an actual diagnosis but a condition that is experienced by many who seek to help others heal. This type of trauma may be experienced by first responders; volunteers; passersby during a natural disaster such as a hurricane, tornado, earthquake, or flooding; or those who come upon a car wreck, a bridge collapse, or another horrific accident.

When secondary trauma becomes sustained, we begin to think of it as compassion fatigue. This is the type of trauma that can be experienced by anyone working over a sustained period with those who have been traumatized. It is also a major and largely unaddressed factor in the burnout that is experienced by helping professionals— mental health personnel working with trauma survivors; direct care staff working in child welfare, substance abuse, developmental disabilities, and poverty programs; and medical personnel. Consider John's story.

> *John volunteered to work on rebuilding homes in New Orleans after Hurricane Katrina. He was retired, felt he had a calling, and liked to work with his hands, something that had previously only been a hobby while he'd worked full-time as a computer engineer. He volunteered in New Orleans as part of a church group. But he was*

unprepared for the devastation he found in the Ninth Ward. Whole tracks of the city were gone, and so many people were scouring the wreckage trying to find some tiny pieces of their previous lives. "I felt the hope drain out of me as I saw the devastation through their eyes," John said. "I remember one older lady just sifting through what was basically rubble. I stopped and asked her if I could help. I took her out to lunch, and she shared the story of her life and her losses of her granddaughter, her husband, and her dog. She sobbed, but there were no more tears for her to shed.

"That night, I had a really hard time getting to sleep, and when I did, I dreamt about lost dogs that were drowning and that I couldn't save. I awoke in a cold sweat, shaking. The next day, I sought out my priest who had accompanied our group for the first week. Crying, I told him of my encounter the day before and of my poor night's rest. He spoke about my compassionate heart and how difficult it is not to take the pain of others and make their pain my own, but how important it is to try to do this, if I am going to be successful in this mission."

John was surprised by this secondary trauma—surprised because he was there to help. Instead, he found himself profoundly moved by the pain and devastation surrounding him and needed support for himself.

Maddie's compassion fatigue surprised her as well. She'd worked hard for her social work degree, so she was taken aback when she found that going to work in an outpatient clinic was so difficult. Her goal had been to work with children and adolescents, and that is what she was doing. She wondered why she was having so many problems. She finally brought up her concerns when her supervisor spoke to her—again—about being late for work.

"Maddie, you always volunteer for the children with the most difficult behavioral problems. You don't take breaks, and you eat your lunch at your desk. You're burning out! You are suffering from compassion fatigue," was her supervisor's response.

Living with trauma is extraordinarily complicated. It has been variously described as feeling as if you are living on the brink of annihilation; falling through space with no parachute or protective suit or netting; walking on a ledge with your eyes closed; trying to sleep with a crack in your heart; or needing to balance on the edge of a knife walking stiff and straight, for not to do so would result in falling into the abyss. Trauma literally floods our body, mind, and spirit with stimulation—so much so that it can be overwhelming.

Signs of Trauma

Trauma involves clusters of symptoms, not just one or two. Additionally, it's very important to understand that signs of trauma can also be signs of other mental health challenges. We list some of the key signs of trauma here so you can familiarize yourself with these symptoms, but not self-diagnosis. If you are experiencing what you feel may be trauma, it is a very good idea to seek consultation with a mental health professional to determine what is causing your distress and to obtain a diagnosis. A clear diagnosis is a key step in developing a good self-parenting plan, which we will discuss in Part Two.

A traumatic event involving death or a serious threat that you witnessed or personally experienced, or one that you confronted, may result in feelings of intense fear, horror, or helplessness. As a result, you will experience a mix of the following (APA 1994):

- Numbing, detachment, or a lack of emotional responsiveness
- Feelings of being in a daze

- Feeling that things are not real
- Flashbacks or bad dreams
- Feeling outside of yourself, as if you are watching what is around you rather than being part of your life
- Inability to recall key parts of the trauma
- Decreased interest or participation in important activities
- Inability to have a full range of feelings—for example, not trusting those you are close to or being unable to love
- Not having a positive view of yourself in the future, not having confidence in yourself to have a career, marriage, children, or live a long life
- Feelings of dread or doom for no apparent reason

The trauma itself is persistently re-experienced through:

- Recurring thoughts
- Images
- Memories
- Dreams
- Body sensations
- Flashbacks
- A sense of reliving the event

There is a marked change in behaviors compared to before the event. Some of the new behaviors include:

- Significant anxiety
- Difficulty falling or staying asleep
- Irritability
- Outbursts of anger
- Difficulty concentrating
- Hypervigilance
- Exaggerated startle response

As a result, you may:

- Avoid thoughts, feelings, conversations, activities, people, and places that remind you of the event
- Experience significant distress or impairment in social, occupational, or other important activities, which can negatively affect your ability to obtain necessary resources or seek comfort by sharing your distress with family members or close personal friends

The symptoms listed above are indicative of acute stress disorder or PTSD. Complex trauma and C-PTSD have similar symptoms to acute stress disorder and PTSD with these additional symptoms (Herman 1992b; van der Kolk 2003; Maté 2003):

—Changes in mood and behavior, including:

- Ongoing sadness
- Problems in regulating mood and behavior
- Difficulty in developing self-soothing behaviors
- Difficulty in actively protecting oneself
- Self-injury
- Illness—psychosomatic or actual
- Motor restlessness
- Anger that is oppositional, extreme, or inhibited
- Difficulty remembering traumatic events
- Sense of distrust and/or of helplessness
- Difficulty in beginning things
- Shame, guilt, and self-blame
- Sense of defilement or stigma
- Suicidal ideation as a way to solve problems
- Excessive sexual behavior or inhibited sexuality

- Feelings of aloneness and difference from others (may include sense of terminal uniqueness leading to being a person no one can understand; separateness from others; or feeling one has a nonhuman identity)

—Focus on the perpetrator, including:

- Distrust of adult caregivers
- Preoccupation with relationship with perpetrator
- Feelings of having a unique or supernatural relationship with perpetrator
- Adopting the perpetrator's value system
- Thoughts of revenge
- Giving perpetrator total power (note: victim's determination of perpetrator's power may be realistic)
- Thinking of the abuse as a gift because you have grown through it and are grateful for the opportunity to grow

—Problems in relationships with others, including:

- Isolation and withdrawal
- Panic or rage when certain parts of the body are touched
- Distrust
- Discord in intimate relationships
- Putting yourself in situations from which you need to be "rescued"
- Loss of spiritual faith

Summary

Dealing with the impact of trauma, in all of its various forms, is a daily occurrence for many, and the experience of trauma is becoming more pervasive. Most of us will have at least one traumatic experience in our lifetime; many of us will have more than one. Trauma is part of the fabric of human existence, albeit a treacherous piece, one that demands respect and attention—the right kind of attention, which will allow the person to move through trauma's pain and resolve its hold.

Unfortunately, most of us treat trauma as we treat many difficult situations. We feel too busy to be burdened by taking the time required to resolve its entanglements. As a result, we begin to experience layer upon layer of pain as we try to fend it off as best we can.

Our next two chapters will focus on living with trauma and on one of a series of strategies for coping with trauma—one that is fraught with its own perils—codependency.

CHAPTER 2

∾

Living with Trauma

Our deepest fear is not that we are inadequate.
Our deepest fear is that we are powerful
beyond measure. It is our light, not our
darkness, that most frightens us.

—MARIANNE WILLIAMSON, *A RETURN TO LOVE*

Within the darkness of our trauma there is a light, but it is frightening because it threatens to take us from the known—our pain—to the unknown: recovery. Our development of codependency, which we will address more fully in Chapter 3, is a midway point in our journey to recovery. It is our beginning attempt to make sense of what has happened to us and to address what it is we need. We do this in an indirect way, by finding someone, understanding what it is that they need, and giving them what we ourselves need but can't figure out how to give to ourselves: support, caring, and acknowledgment of pain. We do all of this hoping we'll make our own pain recede.

The Many Layers of Trauma

Think of trauma as something that is layered. Much like an onion, each layer is distinct. Each has its own shape and texture. Each has developed due to the environmental factors surrounding and influencing it. And each produces its own special tears.

Some individuals experience only one type of trauma, but other individuals experience multiple levels of trauma over an extended period of time—throughout childhood, adolescence, and adulthood —due to multiple sources. This layering of trauma, a virtual montage, is particularly challenging to tease apart and resolve, and is the perfect breeding ground for the shaping of a person into a caretaker, leading to the development of codependency. Codependency, the close intertwining of two individuals, is the attempt of those who have experienced trauma to seek relationships in which they feel they may have *positive power* to influence the other for good. Those with codependency are often desperately seeking to give what they most want to receive—acceptance, nurturance, and love. Codependency is an attempt to escape from feelings of unworthiness and helplessness and replace them with feelings of personal efficacy, power, and control, as well as the ability to connect positively to another.

Managing Our Feelings

Our way out of codependency is to learn to manage our feelings: easier said than done because to do this we need to first understand what our feelings are. For many, this makes managing feelings quite a challenge, particularly when our feelings are triggered by our previous traumas, when they are not just in response to the here and now, but are also in response to the past (See "Trauma Triggers" later in this chapter). And all of this occurs at the same time.

When triggering occurs, we respond in ways that are largely physiological and not conscious and can feel like an out-of-body experience. When we are traumatized or are reliving trauma, we can literally feel that we have become a *shape-shifter*. Shape-shifters—mythical creatures that can change into animals or other forms—are part of Native-American and Irish traditions (to name just a few). We "shape-shift" by *depersonalizing*, by feeling separate from our body or our experience or both, without being able to influence our body. In doing this we may develop the ability to move outside ourselves and actually see ourselves in a room, perhaps from the ceiling or from the corner of a room, rather than feel ourselves with others and as a part of what is occurring around us.

We can also *dissociate* from our experience and become *time travelers*, segmenting that experience and feeling apart from what is happening, perhaps leading to little or no recall of what we have done. Or we may feel that we are a very different age from our true chronological age. For example, we may feel and problem solve at a three-year-old level, instead of feeling and problem solving at our true age of thirty-three. Both *dissociating* and *depersonalizing* are ways that we *freeze*. As one researcher notes, "Adults with a history of child abuse typically experience a greater tendency to freeze at the moment of subsequent trauma, and to develop dissociative symptoms." (Scaer 2001, 108).

Trauma can also bring about rage reactions, the *fight* response. This is the impulse to attack at the time of the trauma, which is often not acted upon by the child for very good self-preservation reasons. The fight response may be triggered during the reliving of trauma, resulting in what looks to the world like a massive overreaction to whatever the negative event was. And finally, there is the *flee* response: running away from anything—a commitment or a request or a bomb.

The key to managing all three reactions (freeze, fight, and flee) is in how we have learned to manage our feelings. Humans have a tendency to do is what is familiar, even if it is painful. This is why learning to actively take care of ourselves—to *self-parent*—is so vitally important. That is why we offer guidelines, suggestions, and exercises for self-care in Part Two. Whether you use the self-parenting steps, affirmations, and self-soothing exercises alone or in addition to psychotherapy and perhaps even medication, making the decision to self-parent is important. Not only are there trauma triggers to navigate, but traumatic responses are powerful and have the potential to make even simple decisions (such as what supermarket to use) a breeding ground for panic. Trauma has the ability to totally influence how life is seen and how life is lived. So let's take a moment to understand what happens when our trauma is triggered.

Trauma Triggers

Trauma triggers are events or experiences that remind us of our earlier trauma, igniting the feelings that we had when we first experienced the trauma—feelings we may not even have experienced at the time because they weren't safe. Triggers can be literally anything: a word, a look, the way the light moves across our field of vision, a smell.

When we are triggered, our body and mind feel that we are under attack—again. In that moment we may remember a very painful event; something that was said; what we were wearing; the smells, the taste, the feeling of the air on our skin. Or we may just experience sensations in our body or fragments of a memory, and respond with emotions that are powerful, intense, and seemingly come from nowhere. We may be unsure about what is happening (Levine 2010) and attach our responses to the situation we are currently in as we try to make sense of our reaction, convinced it is in response to what has just occurred. We may not even know that we are being triggered. We may just experience intense emotion and decide that those in front of us—our children, coworkers, husband—did something that provoked our response. The good news is that when we begin to feel those earlier feelings and make connections to their origins, we're getting ready to actually deal with them.

Feeling Flooded by Emotions

When we are triggered, we rev up and go on high alert, ready for what we have been conditioned to experience in the past. We may feel ready to either attack or flee, or we may freeze by dissociating or depersonalizing. What is important to remember is "the ongoing cues of the present continue to trigger indiscriminate arousal and fear. The present, therefore, serves only to thrust the victim back into instinctual and conditioned modes of self-preservation. . . ." (Scaer 2001, 205).

Trauma can literally unleash a flood of emotions. The flooding can be so strong that it can momentarily overwhelm our ability to process what is happening, and it can certainly hinder our ability to understand it. When someone is being flooded, she may begin crying about one thing and then blubbering and not making particular sense, and finally speaking about many things. Someone else may get angry at a cup being on the counter, and in a blink of an eye, he is ranting about all sorts of things, many of which may have occurred in the past.

Flooding is an excessive triggering of past trauma that comes up as feeling, body sensation, and perhaps some memory, even if the memory is fragmented. It is intense and largely biochemical (as we discuss in Chapter 5). But flooding leaves us confused, frightened, and often feeling shamed because we cannot understand what just happened.

Blaming Ourselves

It is easy to blame ourselves when triggered events occur. What we need to do instead is understand flooding and how the rest of our trauma is triggered so that we can take actions that keep us safe. Trigger responses are also concerning for whoever is with us when we are triggered, which is one reason why it is so important to understand that we are dealing with trauma: we need to obtain support from those closest to us while not overwhelming them.

We also need to take actions that help us heal. This means that we need to take all of our trauma triggers seriously and not minimize them by treating them more like pesky flies than a real call for attention. We need to stop thinking that the problem is really just us and we should get over ourselves, grow up, fly right, cut the crap, or any other phrase we might use to blame ourselves. We need to stop rationalizing our discomfort by saying that anyone would feel this way— or worse, by denying that we are having feelings. We need to look at the situation we have placed ourselves in and identify whatever it is that is triggering us. And we need to reflect on what is happening so we can see our own progression and come to know that many of these reactions to triggers that started in adolescence were due to an initial trauma that happened in childhood ... or in Iraq ... or during 9/11 ... and have continued.

The Body Knows

Our sensitivity to our environment is both biological and learned; this is compounded by our state of mind at the time that our triggers were introduced (Siegel 1999). Whether or not we are tired, already excited, angry, frightened, overwhelmed, "in the zone," or slightly intoxicated can all influence how we respond to a trigger.

Triggers can be difficult to understand because many of them are not conscious thoughts or clear memories; in fact, many triggers are located in our bodies. We call these *body memories*. They are feelings of dread, panic, fear, or rage that arise when certain parts of our body are touched (even innocently) in play; when we are bumped into on an elevator or on a subway; while we are getting a haircut; when we are making love; and certainly when we are touched in other pro-vocative ways, such as when someone jokingly punches us or puts a hand in our face during an argument (Levine 2010; Maté 2003; Scaer 2001; Seigel 1999).

Daquan would jump any time his two-year-old tried to give him a hug. His baby would hang on his neck, which would make him cringe and cause the baby to cry. At first, Daquan just tried to play it off, tickling his baby to make him laugh, but the feelings of panic only got worst over time. Eventually, with his wife's support, he sought out his pastor. "It feels like he's trying to kill me, choke me. I know this is crazy, but I can't stand him—or anyone, for that matter—touching my neck. Maybe that's why I have dreads, so no barber will come near my neck."

His pastor recommended he see a mental health professional. Daquan went into therapy and began to realize that having grown up in foster homes had a major negative impact on him. He began to sense that perhaps there had been an early threat to his life, one he couldn't consciously remember, but one that his body knew.

External and Internal Triggers

Trauma triggers can come from two sources, *external* or *internal*. External sources include smells, which are a very early way that an infant relates to its environment. A smell can bring back a body memory that may even be preverbal, since memories are captured in neural pathways developed very early in life. An external trigger can also be the mention of a place where you were in a battle or the view of a house or apartment building that looks like the one where you grew up. An external trigger can be a word, like the name of someone who deeply hurt you, or a sound, like an engine backfire that imitates a bullet and brings back terrifying memories. There are numerous ways in which we can be triggered by our environment and those who inhabit it.

Triggers can also be internal, such as a pain in a specific part of the body that causes a memory to come flooding back, or even the touching of a body part that is associated with past trauma. It can even be a bruise that, while innocently acquired by bumping into something, feels like it is burning when we look at it, which makes us feel very unsafe.

Trauma triggers may be experienced in clusters due to any number of major or minor events, resulting in intense stimulation. When this level of being triggered keeps happening, it can begin to feel like "normal." In fact, it can feel so normal that we actually seek out a high level of stimulation (and the adrenaline rush associated with it) and plan our life around making sure that this high level of adrenaline is present. We speak about those who walk around triggered as being *adrenaline junkies*. This can become a neurobiological need as we become biochemically used to a high level of adrenaline. Due to trauma, we can become hardwired to feel we need the adrenaline rush and to seek situations that produce the high level of neural stimulation that accompanies it. We once had a man in one of our retreats who held a record for skydiving around the clock. He self-identified as an adrenaline junkie but framed it by saying that at least now he had a *safe* way to get his adrenaline fix; he was a Vietnam veteran and a retired undercover narcotics officer. He justified his hobby by announcing that his previous pursuits were much more dangerous.

William James, the main character in the stunning movie *The Hurt Locker*, is another example of an individual engaging in dangerous behavior to get a "rush." At the conclusion of the film, James elects to return to war and the thrill he obtains from disarming hidden explosive devices when he realizes that he cannot comfortably fit into family life.

For most of us, there are more subtle ways that we address the same biological needs for high levels of stimulation in our lives, including stressful jobs such as being an ER nurse or a teacher in a violence ridden community. These types of professions also provide a fertile source of possible trauma for us.

Trauma Reenactments

There are other ways that we take on trauma that are less than helpful. Trauma reenactments are the re-creation in adulthood (or even adolescence) of painful scenarios and outcomes that we experienced as a child. Reenactments are unconscious manifestations of our trauma that serve to reconfirm our earlier negative beliefs and often lead to a flood of emotions. Trauma reenactment may set a series of events in motion, events that lead us to conclude that we are indeed unlovable, that we will always be betrayed, that we have to be the ones to fix "it"—whatever it is—or it will stay broken. These well-worn tracks get played out again and again, often in small ways. But even small interactions can leave us feeling that nothing will ever change; that we will always feel as we do right now; that life holds no promise and there are no solutions—because every time we leave this place, we find ourselves right back here again. These feelings can lead to the growing frustration found frequently in adolescents with behavior problems, and to the bitterness and health problems (such as being overweight) found in adults.

Trauma reenactments are ways that we keep our codependency alive and prove to ourselves that we have to be the way we are, that there are no alternatives. And they can be played out in our social circles, in our intimate relationships, or in how we treat ourselves. There are many themes possible with trauma reenactments; we'll examine several of the most common.

Jealousy in Intimate Relationships

Jealousy is often a vehicle for trauma reenactments. We project onto a partner the betrayal of trust that we experienced as a child, and we unconsciously attempt to make the betrayal a reality—not because we are crazy, but because we are trying to create a different outcome. Jealousy is a manifestation of *disrupted bonding*.

Anna, a beautiful young woman in her twenties with flowing blond hair and a highly unusual flair for the dramatic in her dress, is a showstopper whenever she walks into a room. Recently married to Roger, a physician, she is an attorney who specializes in proving the innocence of individuals on death row. She loves her work—the intensity, the literal life-and-death reality she deals with. And she loves the "rightness" of her cause, the ability to make something positive happen where all hope seems lost.

Anna and Roger seem like the perfect young married couple . . . on the outside. Inside, their relationship is another story. Anna is intensely insecure, which comes out as being "insanely jealous," something that always catches Roger by surprise: "She's always the most beautiful woman in the room." If they attend a party, Anna notices who Roger speaks to, and she quizzes him afterward about what was really going on. If he stays late at the hospital, she loses it and rages at him, frequently hitting him, throwing things, and accusing him of having an affair with a nurse.

"My mind races from scenario to scenario, all of them involving his betraying me," Anna says. "I'm tormented by these thoughts. But for me, they aren't just thoughts—they are realities. I love him, but I feel he clearly doesn't love me. This is old thinking for me."

Anna is reenacting the betrayals she felt as a child. As the youngest child by several years, she felt abandoned by both her older sister and brother when they moved away. Anna was left to live alone with her hoarding mother and her weak, ineffectual father who was heavily into porn. Both her parents were emotionally unavailable, which left her feeling alone, unloved, and unseen. In fact, as a child, she found herself staging conversations with her parents to see if they even knew her name.

Growing up this way caused Anna to internalize what was essentially her invisibility and her feelings of not being lovable, something she continues to test with her husband. Her rage responses are more characteristic of a child than an adult and are an indication of how young she was when this trauma began. She counters this by working with inmates who are literally in a life-and-death situation, making sure she is needed and seen. But she struggles to internalize the positive in these experiences because she is hooked on being needed by the inmates (her codependency in action, something we'll explore in the next chapter) and being noticed so she won't be abandoned—again.

Reenacting Trauma with Ourselves

Trauma reenactments can also involve how we treat ourselves, not just how we react to others. In this type of reenactment, we re-create what was done to us.

> *Keira was probably abused from birth. Her mother, a member of the Junior League and many other charitable organizations, had rages that were carefully denied by her father, a bank president. They lived in a beautiful home with lots of help to take care of the house and grounds. This was a family many thought was perfect.*
>
> *Keira's mother beat her on parts of the little girl's body where bruises didn't show. She was routinely locked in a closet. She was threatened with worse if she cried, so she learned to endure the hair pulls and being dragged down the stairs, and she did it with dry eyes.*
>
> *She grew up to be a "gym rat," as she called herself. She spent hours a day working out—playing racquetball, swimming, running —to the point that she began to injure herself repeatedly. At first, Keira thought this was a result of the injuries she had sustained as a child and adolescent. Yes, she had vivid memories of many of those injuries. But later, she realized that she was re-creating what was done to her: re-creating the physical pain, the need to deny the feelings of pain, the need to pretend everything was fine, the need to look good, the need to pretend that everything was good. She would just exercise and dissociate, reenacting her childhood misery.*

Trauma Bonds

Trauma can also be manifested through intense attachments. Those attachments are called *trauma bonds*. They are seen in the relationship between victim and perpetrator where there has been an exploitation of power or trust such as in the famous Stockholm syndrome, where unusual empathetic bonds between some hostages and their hostage-takers or between abused women and their abusers, has been documented. Trauma bonds are also found in the relationship between two or more individuals who have experienced the same trauma (Carnes 1997). Trauma bonds are frequently seen in work situations where two or more individuals support each other in dealing with highly stressful work demands, high expectations, and extremely poor direction from a supervisor.

> *Lourdes feels that under any other circumstances, she wouldn't even like her coworker Jewel, let alone have lunch with her regularly. Yet here they are again, commiserating over the poor leadership provided by the head of their agency who is again changing how records are to be kept. And worse, Lourdes feels that she is somehow responsible for Jewel, that she has to keep going into Jewel's cubicle or texting her so Jewel will keep her cool and not mouth off to their wimpy supervisor and be written up—again.*
>
> *Lourdes feels incredible pressure to make sure Jewel isn't fired, and it is wearing on her and her ability to get her own work done.*
>
> How did I wind up here? *she wonders.*

Lourdes has bonded with Jewel due to the very difficult work circumstances that they find themselves in. It is not unusual for individuals in certain situations to find support in people with whom they may not have found much in common otherwise. But Lourdes has taken this one step further. She actually feels responsible for Jewel, and this is compromising her ability to be productive in her own work. Her trauma bond has now moved into codependency, where she is not just bonded with a coworker but is also responsible for her.

Alcohol and Drugs

When we discuss trauma and its impact on our lives, we must look briefly at alcohol and drug use and their biochemical impact on someone with trauma. A note of caution: *Alcohol and drug use, even in moderation, can accelerate some individuals' traumatic responses.* For those of you who are actively dealing with trauma, this note of caution is important enough to repeat: even small to moderate amounts of alcohol or a drug can dramatically intensify the trauma responses of dissociating, depersonalizing, rage, terror, or needing to run (NIAAA 2011; Evans and Sullivan 1995). We'll discuss this in more depth in Chapter 5, The Neurobiology of Trauma.

Jillian, a surgeon who specializes in pediatric cardiology, is an example. She recounts how learning of her husband's latest affair has profoundly altered her life, including her social drinking.

To go through a day, and certainly a night, I need to remind myself that I'm navigating a minefield. The sad reality is that as I try to move forward, which is quite an accomplishment in itself, I must pay attention to the trip wires in my emotional landscape from my childhood. If I don't, I'll touch one, feeling surprised that it's still there as it blows up literally in my face. I need to monitor my thoughts, keeping at bay those that will send me into a tailspin. I also need to be aware of my actions so I do not take out my anger on myself.

I go through a day being both four and thirty-five. Yes, I do tend to underestimate the impact that my traumas have had on me. I'm so self-reliant, almost compulsively so, that I keep being surprised by how vulnerable I actually am. I keep thinking that I should be over my childhood by now. That I should be able to shake this off, live a "normal" life. But I'm gradually coming to realize that I'm not over my past. The latest betrayal by my husband literally ripped the scabs off all the traumas I had experienced as a child, scabs that covered areas that were healing and now are as inflamed, raw, and oozing as if they just occurred. And in some ways they did.

And I can't even look forward to that occasional glass of crisp, cold wine anymore. I realize that I've flipped out too many times after just a glass or two. I realize that I need to gain some control in my life. I feel like I'm living in pieces. I'm a heart surgeon, and I can't even heal my own heart. I'm so overwhelmed. Somehow I have to make myself whole again.

Summary

Trauma can be the unconscious motivator in the lives of those experiencing this legacy of devastating events. Living with trauma is complex and takes a toll on the individual, potentially shaping even small decisions. From the experience of having one's trauma triggered by subtle cues in the environment to actually developing scenarios in one's life where the devastation of trauma is unconsciously reenacted, trauma remains with us, influencing us at every turn. As a result, it also influences how we define ourselves and how we relate to others, as you will see in Chapter 3.

CHAPTER 3

∾

The Codependency Connection

Crisis is opportunity.

Codependency is a type of *attachment* to another person, an organization, or a cause in which we place a greater value and priority on his or her needs than we do on our own. The reason why we learn to attach in this particular way often begins very early in life. As young children we need attachments to survive. Our vulnerability creates a situation where we need to be able to depend on those around us, so we attach to others, even if there are problems with how well the caregiver can give us what we need.

When we attach to a caregiver whose caring is unpredictable or unreliable, we attach in a manner that is less than ideal for our future development (Siegel 1999); we may experience anxiety and possibly rejection surrounding the fulfillment of our basic needs. If our needs haven't been fulfilled, or if they have been fulfilled to some degree but combined with anger, anxiety, and rejection, we still continue to need. We're children, remember, so what other choices do we have? But this portends problems later in life.

As adults, our needs don't go away just because our bodies grow. We still need others, so we develop relationships in a manner that makes sense to us, that makes it possible for us to take care of ourselves in the way that we know best. If being cared for also means being demeaned, rejected, or made anxious, then this whole package is what we will look for in another, because on some level—perhaps a preverbal level—we "know" this equates to having our needs met. And for some, this becomes a personal definition of love.

The Creativity of Codependency

Codependency is a creative solution to the problem of having our needs met. On some very deep level, we know that we need more than we are receiving. But we go about it in a very indirect manner. We become creative in the way we give to others. Many adults, and some adolescents, develop a need, a passionate desire, to literally give to another (or to an organization or cause) what *they* most need: support, love, nurturing, acceptance, commitment, even sacrifice. In essence, they *displace* their needs onto others. They learn to give, unconsciously, in the hope of receiving what they need. And unconsciously, they hope to accomplish this without all the pain they experienced as a child. When that doesn't work, they give more and more, until they lose themselves in the other person, mission, or organization.

And when they crash, as they inevitably do—when the partner for whom they have sacrificed so much leaves them, or they feel that their kids hate them, or they find themselves being trashed on

Facebook—they suffer again. They become ill, act out, get fired, gain weight, drink too much. Life feels like it is in chaos. And yet, this also feels strangely familiar, and they are confident that they can handle it.

Codependency is an attachment that often looks good to others: "Do you see how she dotes on him?" . . . "She's so very dedicated, the agency is lucky to have her as their CEO." But it is a very expensive type of attachment because it costs a great deal for those with codependency to care for the other person or the cause. It costs them their self-care, because the other person or cause inevitably becomes more important than they are.

Codependency: A Positive Adaptation?

Most of us certainly began our codependency with positive intentions. There are other ways that we could deal with trauma that are much less positive; for example, we can act out our rage against ourselves by putting ourselves into self-degrading situations such as high-risk sexual encounters or by becoming depressed; or we can act out against others by manipulating conflicts at work or in our families by stealing, by damaging the property of others, or by dealing drugs. Codependency begins from a very good place within us: the part of us that empathizes, has compassion, knows difficulties or pain. It comes from the need to work hard for what is deemed important, a knowledge born of experiencing betrayal and pain firsthand—of knowing trauma.

Codependency is, in many ways, the ultimate gesture in making lemonade out of lemons, but it is one that is costly for the person with codependency and one that ultimately may not prove helpful for the receiver. But we with codependency persevere, all with the ultimate goal (even if it is largely an unconscious goal) of proving our lovability and our capability. We hope that by doing more, we can earn what we so desperately need.

Because we have a personal understanding of how it feels when someone withdraws when we desperately want to be rescued, or what it's like to attack and need to be forgiven, we are well-suited to navigate the upsets and betrayals that come with an unhealthy connection. This is our own personal dance of intimacy, and our codependent actions can play out in any number of ways.

Learned Helplessness

Developing the ability to so focus on others is a skill, one of many required to survive and even thrive in an environment filled with trauma. One of the drivers of this ability to be so hyperfocused, to be very sensitive to our surroundings, is the need to detect any threat; the goal here is either preventing any potential threat from causing harm, reducing its impact, or redirecting its thrust. This exquisite sensitivity, also called *hypervigilance*, requires an intense *focus outward* on people, places, and things that inhabit the world around us.

With so much focus outward, what can suffer in this equation is the development of inner knowledge. If this imbalance continues, we have a dynamic where we become so attuned to what is outside of us that we do not develop the resources to know what is inside of us: our needs, feelings, wants, and desires. In essence, we learn to be *helpless* about ourselves as we become increasing *helpful* to those around us. When this happens, we are developing *learned helplessness,* another term for codependency (Oliver-Diaz and O'Gorman 1988; O'Gorman 1994).

But hypervigilance isn't all negative. The ability to be extraordinarily sensitive to others can have many positive adaptations in adulthood and result in some interesting career choices. Certainly policemen and soldiers possess this skill. But they are not alone. Good mental health professionals, counselors, educators, child welfare staff, substance abuse and medical staff, to name just a few, are intensely sensitive, and that can be a good thing. The problem is when the focus is only outside and not also turned inward to allow us to get to know and protect ourselves. With all our creative energy going into caring for others and not keeping some major part for ourselves, we become out of balance and develop codependency.

Shame

Intense shame is a common feeling for many with codependency. And its origins begin early. When children experience a parent's withering anger or lack of involvement with them, they believe the reaction has been provoked by some action on their part. They begin to internalize this apparent disapproval, often attaching it to their self-worth. As children and adolescents develop, they more consciously blame themselves for their parent's or caregiver's anger or withdrawal. Shame begins as a concrete attempt to control the pain caused by the disapproval they feel. They may conclude that there was something fundamentally wrong with them, so wrong that it caused the person they so needed as a child not to be there for them emotionally (and perhaps physically) in a way that supported their growth and development. Shame is a result of early emotions tied to disruptive early attachments (Fogash and Copeley 2008).

Shame-based codependent behavior may take many forms. Sexuality is one example, as with a woman who is very eager to please her partner but can't allow herself to achieve orgasm. Her own shame about her body or needs may keep her from sexual fulfillment. But this is compounded by her desire to be wanted, to be considered exciting, and to be needed by another sexually. This could lead her to keep the focus of her efforts on her partner's desires and not explore her own. Another way that shame is manifested is in the need to appear less smart, less beautiful, or less talented than one is to avoid rejection by one's peers, a common concern for adolescents. Individuals who react this way often feel that these gifts are more of a burden because they are distinguishing and cause others to feel uncomfortable, which can lead to rejection. That is exactly the opposite of what someone with codependency needs and wants.

Dealing with shame and fighting against it propels the individual to adopt many behaviors to disprove the shame. And getting hooked emotionally into needing to prove one's worth by having the power to rescue another begins to look an awful lot like codependency.

The Codependency Dance

Codependency takes at least two people performing carefully choreographed steps in their relationship, steps that become well rehearsed over time. Much like ballroom dancing, where there is the leader and the follower, in the codependency dance there is the overfunctioner and the underfunctioner.

Codependency is often expressed as *overfunctioning* in a relationship: one party does most of the work, takes most of the responsibility, and feels most of the pressure. Of course, that requires a partner who is *underfunctioning* in the relationship to make this work. The underfunctioning partner typically feels that the other is responsible for the relationship's stress and strains, even normal ones, and doesn't feel the pressure to stretch out of his or her comfort zone to change, be creative about developing solutions to existing or looming problems, or exert him- or herself to make things work. There may be a feeling of entitlement, and as a result he or she is put out when asked to do simple things to support living together, such as taking out the garbage. This can cause the person with codependency to feel eternally grateful when even simple things are done for them—for example, when his or her partner does even a small thing like making lunch or a friend offers to share class notes.

This codependency dance is a perfect setup for the person with codependency to eventually crash. And it certainly is a ripe situation for the development of feelings of disappointment and even rage. Fiona's story illustrates the development of her codependency:

Fiona came to the United States from the United Kingdom. As a grandchild of Holocaust survivors, she was determined to leave the stories of World War II behind her. Bright, attractive, and ambitious, she was excited about the life she would create for herself. She landed a position in a major publishing house where she quickly rose through the ranks and became an editor.

One day in the hallway she met Ted, a mystery writer just leaving a meeting with his editor. It was love (or shall we say lust) at first look. "Instant connection," she mused with a smile on her face after he asked for her card.

What could be wrong? *she thought.* We both love books, he loves writing, I love editing. We're a perfect match! *They began to spend much of their free time together, usually at her apartment as she had a steady income and he was living on his advance.*

She would make elaborate dinners, sometimes based on takeout due to the long hours she worked. They'd share a bottle of wine, discuss poetry, or the latest theme in his book. It was thrilling.

Eventually, to save money, Ted moved in with her. Ted became more demanding, and Fiona became more accommodating. "He really does have to finish the book," was her justification. But things didn't go well. When she'd ask Ted about progress on his book, he'd become evasive, annoyed, and attack her, saying that if she really cared about him, she'd "actually make a meal instead of just relying on takeout." Fiona would retreat behind these attacks by finding another blog where he could post some material to showcase his writing ability. She also encouraged Ted to set up a website, although she did much of the work on this herself.

One day, everything came to a head. As she tried to revive their sagging sex life by placing an arm around his neck and trying to nuzzle him, Ted called her fat. Fiona tearfully ran from the room and looked at herself in the mirror. The truth was that she had gained weight. She had been eating more, and she had stopped going to the gym so that she could show Ted she loved him by actually cooking for him. She went back to the living room to apologize to him and tell him she would change.

Ted stormed out and didn't come home that night, or the next one either. Fiona was distraught, collapsing because she couldn't determine what else she could do to show him that she cared.

Fiona was clearly overfunctioning in this relationship. She had assumed responsibility for most aspects of their lives and his future, as Ted withdrew behind his book. The more she did, the less he had to do. The more she did, the more he expected. And as she did more, she compromised any constructive pressure for him to gain satisfaction by actively contributing.

This is the dilemma of the codependent relationship—the more one does, the more the other expects. Both parties become increasingly dissatisfied. The codependent partner becomes exhausted from doing more and more, and she begins to have less to give her partner emotionally. Her partner, used to having his needs taken care of, begins to feel abandoned. Both become resentful. Over time, this dance becomes a no-win situation.

We need to remember that everything we have described relative to codependency describes most adolescent relationships. What is a stage for most adolescents can become a permanent behavior pattern for adult children of alcoholics and children of trauma. Adolescence is an excellent time to intervene in this type of codependency pattern, but rarely do parents or guidance counselors recognize this behavior for what it is—incipient codependency.

Compulsive Self-Reliance

In this form of codependency, the focus of attention is usually on a cause, not on another (unless the codependent feels they must be superheroes and keep rescuing those who surround them). This need to have mastery and control over one's life and to *not* need anyone or anything is a fairly common response in those who have experienced trauma. Their hyperattention and hypervigilance are focused on their store, agency, factory, corporation, platoon, organization, patients, or students, with their feelings of self-worth rising or falling depending on how effective they are in achieving their goals. They are focused high achievers who expect to get their self-worth from what they can accomplish. Unfortunately, this form of codependency—of being so very resilient, so very powerful, masterful, and dedicated—can literally kill you. (Oliver-Diaz and O'Gorman 1988; O'Gorman and Oliver-Diaz 1990). Through overwork and a lack of self-care, those with this type of codependency can get to a point where they ignore weight gain or loss, symptoms of diabetes, and even signs of a heart attack, because they are too busy, too needed.

Compulsive self-reliance is frequently a coping skill that receives a tremendous amount of praise because it is so dramatic and can be even heroic at times. This is often the case for those the world decides to love—for example, leaders like Abraham Lincoln, Nelson Mandela, or Mother Teresa, whose private pain was often ignored. We see their accomplishments and not what it cost them to be so very accomplished. The problem for people who develop compulsive self-reliance is that they begin to believe their own press releases. Their identity gradually begins to merge with their competence. But not just any competence: it is their skill to make things happen, do good in the world, and be powerful. This usually proves to be a precarious situation for them personally.

And their competence gradually becomes not just a part of who they are, but *all* of who they are. They are the Joan of Arcs who go through life in full battle gear ready to defeat any foe, anyone who poses a threat of injury to one of theirs. They are always prepared to do the right thing, but (unfortunately for them) are rarely prepared to be vulnerable. After all, vulnerability would distract them from their mission. So routine doctor visits are forsaken, dinners with spouses or friends are postponed, trips to the gym are canceled, and even the book club that meets only once a month never fits into the schedule. What is important is their work. After all, people depend upon them.

Many of these compulsively self-reliant people are men. Men are celebrated in our culture and in our literature as the lone wolf, the *über*male who is very powerful but ultimately unavailable. Their unavailability makes them particularly attractive to women, especially women who want to please others, women with codependency. In this way, people with codependency can meet and even join together, and both will stay miserable.

Compulsive self-reliance in women can also be found. Although our society still has problems with women who amass power, many women do throw themselves into their work, often to the exclusion of developing other parts of their life. "Soccer moms" are one example; they are supermoms, women who devote themselves exclusively to children, family, and community well-being, sacrificing their own educations or careers, and are then often criticized for being so very "controlling." This makes their compulsive self-reliance look more like self-sacrifice, even if they are feeling the same quiet desperation as their male counterparts.

Remembering or just feeling key moments from the past and trying to run from those memories or feelings by busying themselves, distracting themselves, or trying to pump themselves up is frequently the compulsive self-reliant's reaction to previous traumas. As a result, they try even harder and work with increasing ferocity.

For both men and women, this form of codependency—compulsive self-reliance—can be a brittle response to trauma (Oliver-Diaz and O'Gorman 1988; O'Gorman and Oliver-Diaz 1990; O'Gorman 1994).

Codependent Compulsive Self-Reliance as Heroism

Sometimes we become so impressed by the bravery of someone's actions that we fail to see what the cost to them has been. This is particularly true with our military personnel and returning veterans. We see their contributions, we admire their bravery, but we do not often recognize how profoundly their experiences may have shaped them.

Jake returned from his third tour in Afghanistan to a pretty, happy wife and a new baby boy. It was a wonderful homecoming. Everyone from his hometown in rural upstate New York turned out.

Jake, a sergeant, is actually pretty shy. He loved seeing everyone but didn't like the attention. All through the big welcome home party, his mind kept drifting as he wondered how his men were doing. It had been a rough deployment. Several of his men were injured; a few had been killed. That kind of loss left its mark on everyone, but Jake felt responsible. They were, after all, his men. He couldn't get them out of his mind.

In the following days, Jake decided to call a few of his men. He began to visit those he was closest to. They were having their own struggles in the readjustment to civilian life. Jake started offering advice, helping one keep his marriage together, helping another one deal with an aging parent, referring a third to the VA for treatment of what looked like PTSD. Soon his days and nights were filled with talking to and seeing "his men."

His wife has grown resentful; this wasn't the homecoming she had anticipated. And she worries that he isn't spending much time with his new son. But his men are grateful that they still have his solid support and his steady leadership . . . and his neighbors and friends admire his heroism and dedication.

Jake is so focused on caring for his men that he isn't focused on caring for himself or his wife and new son. He needs to be reassured that his men can use the skills they learned in the military to navigate civilian life . . . and that he can as well. He needs to learn to let go and begin to focus on his own needs and wants.

Codependent Compulsive Self-Reliance as Awe-Inspiring Commitment

Sacrifice can be an important element in how codependency plays out in one's life. Someone who has lived with trauma understands how unfair life can be. Many who go on to develop codependency try to rectify life's unfairness in both small and personal ways and in some major ways, trying to affect larger systems that impact areas of life that they know are important. In this way they give their suffering meaning, which is a powerful way of transforming pain, an important resiliency skill. Setting out to change both one's personal world as well as larger systems can be described as heroic, altruistic, and awe-inspiring. You'll see these actions demonstrated by CEOs who literally live and die for their agencies and by dedicated staff who work long, tortuous hours.

When Mark, who we met in Chapter 1, was asked as an adult why he hadn't shared details with his mother about his stepfather's molestation, he said that he didn't want the family to become economically unstable again. They finally had a place to live. His mother and sister were happy. He was protecting his mother and his sister by his sacrifice of silence. He was caretaking them—at great cost to himself. And he was proud that he could do this. "I didn't feel that it cost me much to keep silent. I actually felt worse when I told someone. I felt like I wasn't a man if I couldn't take it. And at age thirteen, I felt I needed to be a man."

Even as a child, Mark was committed to keeping his family together. As he matured, he tried to protect his family from the poverty they had previously experienced. He realized that if he kept quiet, things would continue to be "better" for his mother and sister. And if life wasn't good for him, well, that he could deal with, until of course he couldn't. But his limitations didn't keep him from trying. He was very heroic in his attempt to protect his family, even though it cost him dearly. His adolescence became the training ground for his codependency.

Mark's codependency profoundly affected his career choice. He chose a career in education, specializing in working with kids like he had been: poor and disadvantaged. He was committed to making changes in the lives of those who were like him—the most vulnerable. "I understand what kids go through," he explained. "How tough it is for them. That's why I decided on education as a career choice. And someday, who knows, perhaps I'll be a principal and have my own school."

This is a resilient response from Mark, and a commendable one. After all, it was his teacher who saw the change in him and helped him get back to being the best that was in him. It is understandable that he would want to follow this model, as long as he can navigate this on his terms so that it proves to be a productive choice for him, not just for the children with whom he empathizes.

Codependency can often be seen in those who take on huge, often heroic challenges, and in so doing, burn themselves out. Let's look at Mark's story in a different way. Instead of developing a resilient response, Mark develops a codependent one. Let's fast forward twenty years: Mark obtains his master's in education administration and is now a principal in a charter school. He works incredibly long hours and rarely takes a vacation. He did eventually marry, but his wife sees him as emotionally distant yet strong. He has three children who he rarely sees because of his work commitments. He and his wife are at odds because he's never home. "And when he is home," his wife says, "he's not there anyway."

Mark, to his credit, is aware of this. "But I feel I just have to make this system work for the kids in my school. It's too important for them. There's no other safe place for many of these kids. And I feel that change is just around the corner, if only I can hang on."

Codependency Traps

We usually fall into a codependency trap because we are being routinely triggered at a low to moderate level, and we're not paying attention to what our emotional responses are. When the trauma trigger level is major, it usually gets our attention. This is why we are surprised to find ourselves in a situation that we often have vowed never to enter again, and why we didn't see it coming. Codependency traps are usually situations in which we find ourselves that are familiar.

Mark is in a *codependency trap,* a circumstance that is usually of our own making that literally consumes us. These traps are often situations where we feel we have no alternative but to keep doing what is needed because it is important, even if it is not good for us. These types of circumstances include staying at a job or in a field of work that is eating us alive; becoming overly involved with a friend who is on a self-destructive path; agreeing to caretaking arrangements of others, such as elderly parents, which require too much of us; staying in a relationship that is not supportive of our own needs but one in which we know how to take care of the other. Any of these can trigger our own trauma.

And while there may be times in life where this kind of sacrifice is required, we should strive to make them temporary, not permanent, situations. If this is a constant state of affairs then there is a problem, and the problem is not in the other but within us. Something is triggering us to stay in a situation that is actively not good for us. In fact, many codependency traps are actively harmful.

What makes it a codependency trap is that it is familiar. We know how to do this! We know how to overly focus on another and block out how we feel, which we may do professionally or personally. We know how to navigate a risky landscape (emotional or physical) and keep the goal primary, putting ourselves at risk if need be without even being cognizant that we are doing so. It may hurt to do this, but it is a hurt that in a funny way is comforting because it is so very familiar. This is territory we have walked before. This is the re-creation of the internal emotional landscape that we may have experienced as a child or adolescent. This is our unconscious attempt to experience old traumas again and try to give them a different outcome.

They are traps because we do not see a way out except to do more of the same of what is usually not working. Einstein is quoted as saying that doing the same thing over and over again and expecting a different result is insanity. The good news is that this is a type of insanity where we hold the *get out of jail free* card. We can change our behavior and no longer be trapped. But we have to first realize that we put ourselves there, and we can take ourselves out. And we begin by understanding why we have put ourselves there to begin with.

Feeling Burdened to Act in a Certain Way in Relationships

Sometimes we feel that we must keep playing the same role in life, almost as if it is part of our DNA. As we begin to have awareness of this, it can actually feel like a burden. That insight may not help us change, and so we continue to do the same things again and again that haven't worked for us in the past. In this way, we keep *reenacting* some early belief about ourselves and re-creating an early role that may have worked well for us as a child but may not serve us as an adolescent or adult.

Tracey feels the world is a hostile place for lesbians. She is not feminine, so she feels that she stands out. She feels people are uncomfortable around her in general, and especially when she takes her daughter to the playground. She never seems to be able to maintain a conversation with the other mothers. As a result, she feels isolated and alone, just as she felt as a child. She just doesn't fit in. She can't discuss baking tips; she doesn't bake because she's always worried about her weight. Speaking about husbands is obviously a nonstarter. There just isn't any common ground.

The same dynamic is true for her at work. People just seem to play keep-away. But if there is a mechanical problem with something in the building and maintenance can't be found, or the computers act up and I.T. isn't available, then Tracey is the go-to person. And she hates it, but she doesn't feel she can say anything, because then she wouldn't have any interaction with anyone at all.

Tracey's isolation is painful. And to some degree, it is self-inflicted. She keeps re-creating the rejection and aloneness that she felt as a child. She is awkward navigating the social structure at work and at the playground, so she keeps to herself and doesn't risk trying to make connections with others. But she also feels she's held hostage at work, so she keeps doing what others ask without taking care of her own needs; this is her codependency at work. Her only bond is with her young daughter, which will, at some point, portend conflict for both of them.

Toxic Loyalty

Toxic loyalty is a type of attachment where a person with codependency forms an intense bond with someone to whom she stays committed, despite the negative consequences to herself. This is a very expensive type of attachment because it literally costs the codependent a great deal to stay in the relationship, so much so that this attachment can be seen as toxic to her well-being.

Toxic loyalty can be found in many relationships. It can be seen between a father and son where the son is fiercely protective of his father—even though his father continues to disappoint him. Even if the father continues to miss visitations due to his drinking, the son is convinced his father is going to show up, and the son becomes angry if anyone tries to tell him to go out to play. Toxic loyalty also can be found in many relationships where one partner continues to be unfaithful while the other partner believes that it won't happen again. This couple stays together even though the wounded partner begins to be eaten alive by anxiety. The wounded partner rationalizes that this is the commitment that comes from being in love, when in fact it is more of a toxic bond. Toxic loyalty also can be found in the blind devotion that some people have to a destructive supervisor or agency head, even in the face of increasingly demanding or even irrational behavior that places unnecessary burdens on the staff.

FALLING IN TOXIC LOVE WITH POTENTIAL

Toxic loyalty also can manifest when someone with codependency tries to control either a specific outcome within a relationship or the trajectory of the relationship, or even the trajectory of the life of her partner. Toxic loyalty can be a recipe for disaster for the relationship itself, particularly when the person with codependency works like crazy to ensure that her partner's potential is realized, but her partner isn't so sure that's what he wants. This is a recipe for creating resentments that can lead to the unraveling of the relationship while the person with codependency actually compromises her own well-being.

Lola is a survivor of a violent alcoholic family. She prides herself on being positive about life. A self-described "go-getter," she likes challenges and feels that her life has prepared her for tackling them, whatever their presentation.

Lola met Stephen, a talented but unfocused young musician, and she fell in love with the Stephen she knows he could be. She sees his potential, his passion, and his talent. Lola tells her friends that she's "crazy in love with Stephen."

She sent links from his website to prestigious music blogs, hoping they would post some of his work. She encouraged him to practice, getting annoyed (but trying to hide it) when Stephen didn't work according to the schedule she set up. She frequently brought meals to his house so he wouldn't have to leave his music to travel to hers.

Stephen became annoyed and resentful of the demands she made and her intrusions into his life. He didn't like her high expectations. He enjoyed his life the way it was and didn't see what was so wrong with it. But he really likes Lola, her spunk, her commitment to him. The attention is rather flattering after all. So he didn't end the relationship; they just began to argue all the time. And he began to have affairs, which Lola learned about by going through his texts on his phone while he showered. She found one string of texts from a singer who he worked with and another from a married woman who had broken up with him but with whom he was trying to reconnect.

Lola was thunderstruck. In an odd way, she felt she understood what he was doing, the intense push-pull, the ups and downs. It was painful but familiar, much like her own family of origin, but she wanted to remain with Stephen. She felt they had a partnership that involved their relationship and his music. Lola tried to convince herself that staying would be "the sacrifice one makes for love. And Stephen is so very talented. What a waste if he didn't do something with it." She was convinced he wouldn't do anything with it if she left.

Lola confronted him. He couldn't say why he had been involved with other women, but Lola was devastated. "I gave so much. He is so selfish," was her summation. And now she doesn't know what to do with herself. "I feel like such a failure, that I've failed him and myself. And I'm really worried about what will happen to him and to his music."

Lola and Stephen's relationship was doomed from the start. She invested so much of herself, outside herself, that she was oblivious to the impact her actions were having. Instead of accepting Stephen and developing a relationship with the person he was, she felt she could be more valuable to him if she helped him develop professionally, something he wasn't so sure he wanted to do. He rather liked his life as it was; it wasn't as exciting as Lola wanted, but it was comfortable and safe. It was good enough for him.

In this way, people with codependency can actually sabotage the close, personal connection with another that they desperately want by developing a bond to what the person could be, not who they are . . . and then wonder why the person doesn't reciprocate. This often plays out when we are choosing a life partner, but it can also be seen in relationships with a supervisor, with coworkers, and with the people we may serve or with causes we are committed to.

TOXIC FRIENDSHIPS

Toxic loyalty can also be seen in adolescence, when intense, powerful bonds are formed between peers where one seems to be obviously taking advantage of the other. The disadvantaged adolescent remains staunchly loyal to this peer or group, often to the chagrin of parents or even teachers, who can't quite figure out what the attraction is.

Chelsea felt incredible loyalty to the "mean girl" group at her high school. She was literally their gofer, bringing condiments to the lunch table, picking up books or papers they dropped. She even dressed as they did, even though some of the styles were not becoming on her. One of her teachers became increasingly concerned that Chelsea would do "anything" to fit in and wondered just how far she would go. Things came to a head one day when Chelsea stole a car and picked up the group after a cheerleader practice.

On probation and receiving counseling, she was able to begin to understand that her intense desire to be accepted came from her feelings of worthlessness as a child due to her parents' divorce and remarriages and additional children. "I felt like I was the mistake, like I never should have been born. My parents are both happier without each other, and without me."

Chelsea's deep feeling of unworthiness played an important role in her attaching to this peer group at any cost. She felt that if she could take care of them, they would take care of her, and she'd belong, somewhere.

Toxic loyalty can result in many painful choices. We remain committed to a person or a cause until it begins to turn toxic and threatens to destroy us. We fall in love with potential and become resentful if that person or cause doesn't work to help create the image that we have. We remain committed to helping a sibling who is in reality literally drinking himself to death, or we keep a friendship with someone who continually betrays us yet expects an apology to be sufficient.

What drives our codependency is our fear. We fear we are not enough. We fear that we are only worth what we can give. We fear being alone and abandoned . . . so we stay in toxic relationships, rationalizing that a bad partner is better than no partner because at least we are not alone with just ourselves.

Codependents seek relationships in which they can give what they so need for themselves: a loving attachment. By doing so, they hope to prove themselves worthy, but the cost can be very high. Yet the desire to give, to protect, to take care of someone, is so strong that we've even seen it play out with an inanimate object. Patricia had a client who didn't want to call her answering machine too late. Patricia encouraged her client to call it at any time. "It's only a machine," she said. "It doesn't mind working at three AM." (For a list of ways to tell if your relationship is toxic, visit www.ogormandiaz.com.)

Summary

Codependency is a widely used but an often misinterpreted concept. In essence, codependency is giving to another that which we most want but can't give ourselves: acceptance, connection, love, and understanding. Those with codependency have many positive attributes that need to be recognized. The caring, intelligence, and compassion exhibited are positive attributes that in moderation are extremely positive personality traits. But the problem is that these gifts are not used in moderation. Those with codependency give in the hope that they will receive, but that is rarely the case. Those with codependency often just give and give and give until they are broken and can give no more. They have run on empty for so long that they come close to losing themselves.

The good news is that there are answers to this dilemma. If you are a codependent, you can learn how to parent yourself instead of just parenting those close to you. You can become whole again by making yourself a priority. We'll explore how to do this in Part Two.

Signs of Codependency:

✓ You really need to be needed and aren't in touch with your own needs, so you focus on what others need.

✓ You feel that you have a special ability to understand what others need, so you put yourself in situations where you can take care of others.

✓ You are very sensitive to the cues in your environment but not as sensitive to your inner cues.

✓ You feel that you have to *overfunction* in a relationship if the other person *underfunctions*, so you can keep the relationship.

✓ You rationalize that your *overfunctioning* is okay because you know how to do it.

✓ You believe that if you do more, the other person will appreciate you more.

✓ Your self-worth is tied to what you can do for others; you don't understand what you need to do for yourself.

✓ You rationalize that doing more for others is okay because it's easier for you than it is for them.

✓ You feel more responsible for another than that person feels for you.

✓ You feel attached and responsible for someone else due to your painful shared history.

✓ You believe you have the ability to see the potential or true worth in another and commit yourself to helping him or her maximize that potential.

✓ You fall into the same caretaking relationships time and time again.

✓ You neglect your own care because you can do without.

✓ You take care of yourself last or avoid dealing with your needs because you can wait.

✓ You believe you owe others more than they owe you.

✓ You sacrifice yourself at work.

✓ You dedicate yourself to a cause that demands more from you
    than you can comfortably do, yet you stay with it.

✓ You feel indebted to others who have hurt you because they
    could have hurt you more than they did.

✓ You are committed to others who hurt you because you under-
    stand that deep down inside, they did not mean to hurt you, so
    you deny its impact on you.

✓ You are flooded emotionally and feel alone with your pain despite
    having people around you who need you.

CHAPTER 4

❧

Resiliency and Trauma: Growing Strong in the Hurt Places

A woman is like a tea bag. You never know how strong she is until she gets into hot water.

—ELEANOR ROOSEVELT

L ife can hurt. We all know this. We've all experienced life's challenges and subsequent pain on many occasions. Some of us pray that we will be spared such trials. Others of us hope that along with the trials comes the wisdom to deal with them. Resiliency is another name for that wisdom: the teachings that life can offer us, teachings that often come when we are under maximum stress and in a world of hurt. And the good news is that this wisdom comes from within us.

Trauma is often overwhelming. It can feel almost impossible to make sense of; it can feel so dense that it appears to be impenetrable.

And trauma has power: the power to trap us or to change us. We begin to learn how strong we really are through our resiliency. And when we make resiliency a conscious goal—embracing our strong places, nurturing them, and allowing them to grow—we begin this journey in earnest, and our recovery has begun. As we look back, it is interesting to note that most of our successes have come from our resiliency.

Resiliency is not produced because of the trauma, but is a product of the effective ways in which we manage and eventually master our traumas. We develop resilience by creating internal emotional and psychological scaffolding, an inner structure with steps and resting places that allows us to put our trauma and codependency in a certain place within us where it can be both understood and contained.

Resiliency is the pathway through the pain of trauma and codependency to where our hope is located: within ourselves. We each possess a way of creating a course through our trauma and codependency, one that will allow our healing to begin and to continue. Resiliency is our positive response to a trauma and its resulting codependency, a true positive adaptation that allows us to begin to make sense of it all. It's what we do to actually support ourselves with the cards we have been dealt.

Understanding and containing our trauma and codependency are important steps in developing the skills we need to manage both. Understanding allows us to have access to our trauma and codependency but not to be totally consumed by them. And trauma and codependency can be—and need to be—contained and managed with time, caring, persistence, and optimism. When we do this, we can begin to use the new and emerging part of ourselves as a source of growth and learning. This is our resilience.

In this way, trauma and codependency become catalysts for personal growth. While it is certainly not the type of catalyst we would wish on anyone, including ourselves, trauma and codependency can be a type of stimulus, if you will, that demands some kind of response. So if we're going to respond anyway, we might as well make it a nurturing response. And the active cultivation of resiliency is that self-loving response. Resiliency is learning to respond in a way that helps us grow by taking supportive actions for ourselves, both immediate and longer term ones. It is in the learning from our traumas and codependency that we build new skills, new insights, heal old wounds, and protect ourselves in the future; in short, it is how we build resilience.

Becoming Resilient: A Dynamic Process

Becoming resilient is a dynamic process. We are all resilient to varying degrees, depending on our history of skill development in this area and the stressors that surround us. Resiliency is a skill set that is constantly developing and adjusting to the world around us and the circumstances in which we find ourselves. It is not an off/on switch to be flipped on in times of stress. It is more of *a stream of strength* that flows within our soul. Resilience is like a contact sport (O'Gorman 1994). It is a dynamic process that can look different at various points in one's life depending upon what is being responded to. Over time we can settle into certain patterns, certain ways we are most likely to respond when we are faced with adversity. But it is important to remember that they are just patterns, not givens. We can and we do change.

And we do this in many different ways. Sometimes we make adjustments little by little. Sometimes we have major moments of insight caused by great turmoil, through which we can grow exponentially. These are the moments we often describe as "rising to the occasion," when we perform in ways that are not characteristic of us and that might even surprise us. And there are other moments when we get "sick and tired of being sick and tired," and we begin to change gradually and find ourselves doing things naturally that were previously unimaginable. These are all very real moments, and they speak to our capacity to make sense of the often painful events that life hurls at us. We need to own these moments of change; this is our resilience in action.

Resiliency Styles

There are basically six resiliency styles that individuals use at any given point in their lives when confronted with certain situations or issues (O'Gorman 1994). And many individuals possess at least two dominant resilient styles or patterns. But remember: these styles can shift, bend, or change depending on what we are confronting and how we are making sense of it.

Paradoxical

This resiliency style connotes having skills that seem somewhat contradictory, being used only in one part of one's life and not in another; for example, being efficient at the office but not using those same skills at home to make decisions about one's own needs and wants. People who use this type of resilience pattern often feel that they are literally two different people because they function so differently in various parts of their lives.

For those with codependency who operate with this resiliency style, the challenge is to identify the skills from the area of their life that is working well, and then use those skills where they are underfunctioning. This underfunctioning is usually around their own needs.

Stellar

Sometimes people take great pride in the understanding that they have survived a trauma, but they don't move on from this survivorship mode to develop other attributes and an expanded sense of self. They become caught up in seeing themselves as a "star" in this one area of their life. Important? Yes. But stopping one's growth after a trauma doesn't make for a full life. Examples include those who after many years in a recovery process still identify themselves first by the trauma. Instead of identifying oneself as a social worker, mother, husband, opera devotee, farmer, vegetarian, teacher, or dog lover, this type of person still initially self-identifies as a rape survivor or a recovering alcoholic.

Those with codependency who operate with this resiliency style become stuck in this one identity and have difficulty growing into other areas. Their challenge is to grow beyond this sense of survivorship by using the skills that helped them survive their trauma to develop and embrace other parts of who they are today.

Self-Contained

Knowing that one is resilient and wearing this like armor to the exclusion of developing other parts of one's identity is a self-contained resiliency style. Those with codependency who operate with this resiliency style run from their vulnerabilities and protect themselves by working, volunteering, exercising, or participating to an extreme in some other activity.

These are often individuals we applaud for their dedication, tenacity, and selflessness. Their challenge is to create avenues where they can explore their vulnerabilities and get to know those parts of themselves, much like they would do with any new project.

Underdeveloped

The lack of resiliency development is often due to the lack of opportunity. Underdeveloped individuals are those who have been protected from learning to meet life's challenges. Sadly, one example is our adolescents, who often have stressors buffeted for them by their parents; this is demonstrated by the fact that in one generation, we have gone from the teacher being right to parents fighting teachers on their children's behalf.

Many of those with codependency who operate with this resiliency style may not feel that they can affect much in their own lives, but they try to influence the lives of others. Overly involved as they become consumed with the details and dramas of the lives of those they care about, they simultaneously disregard their own needs. Their challenge is to learn to decipher their own needs as acutely and accurately as they do this for their friends and loved ones.

Overwhelmed

With this style, resiliency is present but not currently available due to a recent traumatic event. This is the aftermath of trauma, the feeling of being overwhelmed, out of control, not being able to cope.

Those with codependency who operate with this resiliency style are challenged to remember that feeling overwhelmed or out of control is temporary, that they can and will emerge wiser and with a greater depth of compassion for themselves. For some, losing their ability to function by utilizing their strengths is their wake-up call. They begin to realize that they need to and can take care of themselves, not just everyone else. They need to remind themselves of their strengths even if they do not feel they have access to them at the moment. The vehicle for their growth is the fact that they are in a crisis. And due to being in a crisis, they are in need. This realization can facilitate growth because they cannot escape from the fact that they must let someone assist them—for once.

Balanced

A balanced resiliency style is the goal, the gold standard. Balanced means being resilient when needed and using that resiliency comfortably in one's life. Balanced means having skills to take care of ourselves, using those skills when we need them, and being able to function well on our own behalf, not just on the behalf of others. This is the goal of recovery—to be in balance.

Building Resiliency with Restorative and Reparative Experiences

We build our resiliency, and in this way begin our recovery, when we see the challenges before us as a way of *restoring* or *repairing* our senses of self-worth, power, and efficacy—all of which may have been thwarted by the trauma(s) we experienced. *Restorative experiences* are those that expand our sense of self through giving to others. This is very much what is at the heart of the twelfth step of Alcoholics Anonymous and Al-Anon (a mutual support group for those who have been affected by another's drinking): *Having had a spiritual awakening as the result of these Steps, we tried to carry this message to alcoholics, and to practice these principles in all our affairs.* Members of these fellowships are encouraged to give to others what they have received: hope and a sense of purpose. In sharing those gifts, they heal themselves even more by realizing they have the power to give to others.

We see this process of restorative experiences in many areas of life: a man who grew up without a father volunteers to be a scout leader; a woman whose best friend while growing up was her dog becomes a veterinarian; someone born with a cleft palate becomes a surgeon whose goal is to make children smile.

Reparative experiences are those we give ourselves. This is how we change ourselves and give to ourselves what we most need. This is self-parenting in action. Examples are numerous in our lives once we develop a consciousness of this process. Reparative experiences occur when a man tries to rebuild his life after his wife has had an affair: How does he feel about women? About his wife? How does he learn to trust again? Can he let her back into his heart? Or in the case of a mother who confronts the person who murdered her child: Can she find a way of releasing the rage within her so it doesn't consume her? This is what also occurs when we are fired from a job: how do we repair the part of us that has been wounded and give back to ourselves our sense of purpose and self-worth?

Giving Meaning to Suffering Through Inner Narrative

We both repair and restore ourselves by giving our suffering meaning. We do this in both big and small ways through the creation of an inner narrative—our story about ourselves—that becomes part of our resiliency. This resiliency is shown in how we speak to ourselves; what parts of ourselves we emphasize, nurture, and grow; and how we speak about ourselves to others, including what we post on Facebook, share with our friends, and how we interact at family gatherings. We need to listen and ask ourselves, *Am I portraying the real me? Do my stories repair and restore my sense of worth? If not, how can I make them do so? What added information, what emphasis, would present the best in me?*

Viktor Frankl, a psychiatrist who was imprisoned in a concentration camp during World War II, wrote about this in his book *Man's Search for Meaning* (1946; 2006). Frankl's story is one of incredible hardship and great wisdom. He saw and experienced terrible suffering but also incredible tenacity and hope, which caused him to realize that those who survived had found a way of giving meaning to their suffering. In short, they had found a way to make sense of their experience of the Holocaust, and this allowed them to survive and even thrive in its aftermath. They developed strengths and skills that allowed them to continue their lives in the wake of this horrific trauma. They developed resiliencies that they put to use in other parts of their lives.

The ability to give meaning to suffering is not just within ourselves or our families but also can be found in history. It is present in survivors of the ethnic and religious wars between Bosnia and Herzegovina in the 1990s; in the Rwandan genocide in 1994; and more recently in the genocide in the Darfur region of Sudan. In each part of the world, these traumatic conflicts gave rise to the need to make sense of the suffering and move on from it, while remembering it so that the violence doesn't happen again. This call to resolve trauma and develop resilience is also experienced in the United States, where our efforts to come to terms with the trauma of 9/11 have produced much soul-searching and in some ways a stronger nation.

Consciously Repairing and Restoring Our Sense of Self

Trauma can expand the self-concept of the person, according to Steven Wolin, M.D., and Sybil Wolin, Ph.D., who wrote about this idea in *The Resilient Self* (1993). Trauma forces a person to take one of two actions: the first, although positive and perhaps painful, will force movement in a direction that will ultimately facilitate growth.

The other, which may at first feel safer (and may actually be initially safer), may prove to be ultimately self-defeating.

The Wolins see two choices that those who have been traumatized may make both during and after the traumatic experience. They can *submit* to the negative messages contained in the trauma, agreeing in some ways with the perpetrator that they are, for example, worthless, not deserving of love, deserving of abandonment, or deserving to be demeaned by harsh, stinging words or physical punishments. As they grow older, these rationalizations may turn into excuses for not being cared for: they are not deserving of a call or a tender gesture from someone they love; they don't deserve respect from a supervisor; they don't have contact with their children.

Or those who have been traumatized can *rebound* from the psychological insult that is contained in the trauma and take a very different stand. They can learn to see the trauma, the hurt inflicted upon them, as being about the person inflicting the pain. Instead of seeing the trauma as something they deserve, they view it as something about the perpetrator. The Wolins write about this as "knowing who has the problem." Even young children can know that the adult is the one with the problem, and that the adult's reaction is not about something that the child has done but is about the adult. This is a very powerful understanding of what is occurring, because if the child or adult who was traumatized views the problem as something generated by someone or something outside, then there is no personal responsibility for fixing it! The responsibility of the child or the adult is then actually limited to managing his or her reaction to what happened.

What an incredible thought! If you can focus on yourselves in a moment of trauma then you may take a protective step, or a preventive step, or any one of a number of actions. When you stop blaming yourself for everything that is happening around you, it actually frees you up to be creative and take some risks. And taking risks is where your growth occurs—risks like ending a relationship that is too painful, leaving a job for one that feeds your soul, or setting limits for your children, parents, partner, or boss.

Oddly, one of the ways we may grow is in developing compassion for the person who is causing the problem, as opposed to taking responsibility for his actions. These approaches are very different. One approach allows us to grapple with the fact that his unfairness was about him, and it allows us to be creative about the best way to handle the situation. The other approach bogs us down and inhibits our flexibility, for we are literally trying to control another human being, something that is not in our power.

An example might be when we receive unwarranted criticism at work: we decide how we want to handle it to prove our value, perhaps by focusing differently on the assignment. Another example might be when a husband comes home after a long day at work and a wicked commute and begins complaining about the kids' toys strewn around the house and dinner not being ready. Instead of looking at this as evidence of our inadequacy as a wife or mother, we view it as evidence that he's had a really bad day.

Rachel's husband, Tom, would walk in the door after work and start bellowing about the toys and dinner being late again. Rachel would run around like a crazy woman picking up all the toys and putting on a pot of water so they could have dinner quickly. As Rachel tells it:

> *My father was a narcissistic rage alcoholic. I never thought I'd marry someone like him, but I did. So Tom's behavior would trigger me big-time. But one day, a lightbulb went off in my head, and*

I began to ask myself if it really was all about me. Was it really me Tom was angry at, or did he just come home and vent? I spoke to a close friend who encouraged me to "stop being so codependent" and try something different. I decided to risk it and see, feeling actually pretty brave. It felt like staring in the face of the beast—my father's face.

The next day I took a deep breath and greeted Tom at the door with a smile on my face, even though I didn't feel happy. "Bad day?" I asked him. His shoulders slumped, so I gave him a hug. He laughed. I squeezed him harder. He changed clothes and then played with the kids as I finished dinner. I realized that changing my attitude facilitated him changing his.

Rachel *rebounded*. She redefined the problem and risked seeing it as not about her. In taking this positive step, she was able to resolve the problem. Now some would argue that Tom shouldn't come home this way, that he was still the problem, and that is true. The difference in how this situation was resolved is between Rachel's initial actions, which were rather passive and reactive and codependent, and her current stance, a resilient one, in which she takes the power she has and redefines what happens. Resilient individuals tend to be activists. They try to do something about what is causing them discomfort or concern. They choose not to be victims of their surroundings. Rachel is a good example of this in action.

Children can also rebound from trauma. A child who hears comments that she is "stupid" and a prediction that she "will never amount to anything" does not have to buy into this prediction. She can say to herself, *I'll show you!* By doing this, she takes a highly resilient stance to this unfair and potentially crippling judgment. LaTisha was such a resilient child.

LaTisha grew up in a strong, religious family and was raised by a single mother who worked to support her and her four other siblings. LaTisha, the oldest, was frequently put in the role of second parent where she functioned as well as any eight-year-old child could. But she struggled academically. She just didn't learn as the other kids did. This made her anxious and eventually angry. And it was the anger that her teachers saw, the angry girl who didn't do well in school.

One day in high school, as college application deadlines were approaching, she was told by her guidance counselor that perhaps she should reconsider her goal of being a teacher. "Look, your grades aren't that great. Maybe school's not your thing. How about thinking about getting a job?"

LaTisha became really angry. I've had a job raising four sisters and brothers, and I've done pretty well at it, she thought. But her counselor had a point: her grades weren't that good. She applied to a local community college and started night classes. She discovered that with her siblings being just that much older and classes being just about the work and not about all the other stuff that went on in high school, she did get good grades. She completed a two-year degree and transferred to a state college where she did major in education. Now, she is an assistant principal in a school not too far from where she was raised.

LaTisha didn't agree with the negative messages about her potential that surrounded her. She used her anger to fuel her desire to make her dream come true. After the trauma of being judged as lacking, she *rebounded* and became resilient, and she proved those who wrote her off as wrong.

Developing Skills in the Face of Adversity: Resiliency Traits

The ability to develop skills in the face of adversity begins early in life and continues for the rest of our lives. According to Dr. Marylene Cloitre, director of the Institute for Trauma and Stress at the New York University Child Study Center, and her associates (2000), children who develop resiliency tend to show:

✓ **Persistence**—The child works on something until it is finished, tries to succeed on a task after failing, stays committed to his/her goals, and remains encouraged.

✓ **Goal orientation**—The child has goals that are important to him/her and works hard to accomplish those goals.

✓ **Adaptability**—The child feels comfortable with change, believes there are many ways of seeing things, and can easily compromise.

✓ **Optimism**—The child is usually enthusiastic, cheerful, confident that the future holds good things to come, and optimistic that things will get better in the future.

✓ **Willingness to approach novel events**—The child finds it easy to go to new places, enjoys meeting and interacting with new people.

✓ **High self-esteem**—The child thinks he/she is a lot of fun to be with, that he/she can handle stressful things in life, and likes him- or herself.

✓ **Intelligence**—The child generates creative or novel solutions to unexpected problems or can identify similarities between a new problem and one he/she has already solved.

✓ **Good social skills**—The child can ask for help when he/she needs it, make friends easily and keep them, and not get into fights.

Resiliency Is *Not* a Lack
of Vulnerability

Theorists have argued that resilient individuals are in some ways invulnerable, that they just don't experience trauma, and that there is some constitutional, biological, lucky circumstance that makes some individuals not as prone to trauma as others. This is simply not true.

Those who are resilient have worked hard for it. If they have biological circumstances that complicate their lives, such as a physical illness like cancer or a mental illness like bipolar disorder or depression, their lives can be more challenging than the average person's, but it does not mean that they cannot be resilient. This just means that it may be a little harder for them to rebound from a trauma and codependency because they have to deal with three major issues— trauma, codependency, and biological illness.

So you can be resilient and also be compromised by what is happening within your body. In fact, it is frequently those who have experienced a physical or a mental trauma and who utilize their trauma as a reason to grow who are the ones that expand their sense of self and develop resiliency.

Penny developed breast cancer at the age of thirty-three. She is the "supermom" of a three- and a five-year-old and a caretaker to both of her elderly adoptive parents who she dearly loves. She has a lot to live for.

My own biological parents were killed in a car crash when I was six. I really wanted to live and to raise my own children. But the cancer treatments were awful. The mastectomy hurt, making it hard to cuddle with my own babies. And the chemo and the radiation left me physically ill and depressed with no energy.

But I wasn't going to let the cancer beat me. I did everything I could, which included becoming a great deal more spiritual and a whole lot more grateful for what I do have.

I've been in remission now for three years. I know that I'm a stronger person emotionally, spiritually, and in some ways physically for having gone through this trauma. I just completed the Adirondack 90-miler at Saranac Lake, New York, last Sunday, a three-day paddle on three lakes. And I did it in a boat with other women survivors!

Overwhelmed and Still Resilient

Those who have experienced trauma and codependency and developed resiliency are not invulnerable. As we have been saying, living with trauma and codependency is complicated. Once trauma has been experienced, there remains the potential for it to be re-experienced when triggered. Another trauma can send someone reeling, due not just to the current experience but because of what the impact of that new experience can do to resurrect old wounds.

Resiliency can be overwhelmed during times of intense trauma, with virtually anything serving as a potential trigger (O'Gorman 1994). Due to the onslaught of emotional and physical responses to the trauma, coping skills that have been in place (even for a long time) can be stripped away, leaving one feeling more like the child he was at the time of the initial trauma than the adult he is now. Memories can come flooding back in the form of flashbacks or physical memory sensations in the body.

We see this happen with first responders, returning veterans, and those going through life who just happen to get "hit upside the head" by yet another major trauma. "This is the last thing I expected to happen to me," laments Trudy, for example, who woke up in the emergency room to find out that she had been assaulted and raped.

I'm over sixty years old and a grandmother, for gosh sakes. I've made my peace with all sorts of things: being a returning vet from Desert Storm; shipping out when my kids went off to college; continuing my career as an Army nurse; retiring and specializing in trauma care in the private sector. I also survived emigrating to the United States from Ireland after my father sexually abused me. I've survived a lot.

I was about to get in the elevator of my apartment building when I felt someone behind me, then nothing. I guess I got hit on the head. Now to find out this happened . . . I feel so unsafe. I can't go on an elevator: the smell—it reminds me of what happened. And I have all these doctor visits, and they all involve elevators.

Now I get panic attacks. I wake up afraid that my father is going to lock me out of the house again if I don't do what he wants. And I keep getting that headache I got from the heat in the desert. I close my eyes and I see body parts. I smell the human decay and the hot sand, and I keep hearing the sounds that I thought I left behind. It feels like it's all around me. I want to slap it. I tried doing that in the hospital and they put me on some intense medication. But I guess that's what I need.

They say I now have PTSD. Funny, I didn't have it before. But I sure have it now.

Trudy's reaction is not uncommon. Many who experience trauma can come through it without major, long-lasting problems, but then something else major occurs, and it all comes back with a vengeance. Trudy's early life set the stage for this in some ways. She responded to the early abuse by her father by becoming a professional caretaker.

She cared for soldiers while in the army on deployment, and she specialized in trauma care. And now she is on the receiving end of this type of care. No, she is not a failure. Being so very traumatized doesn't mean that her early coping skills evaporated; her resiliency is just overwhelmed. Rather, this is an opportunity for her to deal with her earlier traumas, and to deal with her response to handling them—her codependency.

Codependency Is Growing from the Outside *In*

Codependency is related to resiliency: it is certainly the development of strengths under pressure. And many aspects of codependency are desirable. In fact, many people unconsciously look for someone who has a codependency skill set when they are looking to develop a relationship. Those with codependency are often seen as special because they are so in tune with others, seeing what they need and understanding the requirements of the current environment. The problem arises when those skills wind up trapping the giver. Codependency involves the active denial of the user's needs, all for the benefit of the other person or cause.

Codependency is an attempt to grow from the outside in. Those with codependency are constantly measuring their self-worth by taking care of the needs they see around them instead of meeting the needs they feel within themselves.

Resiliency Is Growing from the Inside *Out*

Resiliency comprises a different skill set than codependency does, one that is built on developing areas that can help a person who has experienced trauma grow from the inside out. Inside is where the traumas are felt, but what we do with those feelings when we are developing resiliency is something different from what we do when we are developing codependency, both behaviorally and biochemically.

When we learn to be resilient, our traumas are used as launching pads for the development of new skills. Some resiliencies are specific to dealing with our trauma: these include the insight we develop that enables us to self-soothe without resorting to alcohol or illicit drug use; or our ability to know our triggers and use this knowledge to slow down time and not immediately react. Resiliency can also come from our attempts to manage our codependency; our growing ability to set limits, to act out of our own self-interest and not just someone else's; our ability to ask for what we need and not just give someone what *we* need.

Resilient individuals learn to better manage their trauma, use their other skills to engage others positively, enjoy a good laugh, be realistic, and let their innate optimism shine. Resilient individuals tend to be good problem solvers, and may also pride themselves on "giving back" to others who are currently in the situation they were once in. They grow, prompted by their history and stimulated by their present. Their growth is based on their developing an understanding of their needs.

Resiliency: The Codependency Alternative

Resiliency *and* codependency develop due to the same pressures, the same traumas, the same need to make sense out of things that may at times defy reason. But resiliency directs the person inward toward the development of his or her own abilities, toward his or her own needed survival skills. Resiliency is a skill set that allows us to venture forth into the world that we wish to inhabit, acting in our *preferred way* (Eron and Lund 1996).

Resiliency on Steroids: Post-Traumatic Growth

Post-traumatic growth can be viewed as the ability of our brain to respond positively after trauma (Tedeschi, Park, and Calhoun 1998). We know that all through trauma, whether it's a one-time event or sustained over a period of time, the brain is continually trying to make sense of the experience, continuing to learn, and continuing to make connections, as we will see in the following chapter on neurobiology.

Post-traumatic growth is the integration of the traumatic experience that takes place when healing is in earnest. It is not the light at the end of the tunnel. It's being in the tunnel, knowing it's a tunnel, making sense of its contours, and determining a positive direction to literally reach the light. This also is the essence of the Self-Parenting Recovery Plan that we will discuss in Part Two of this book.

Individuals can have a very real epiphany at this point in their recovery. Here is when the B-I-G *a-ha* moments occur, when we begin to realign our actions and our beliefs. This leads to breakthroughs consisting of new behaviors, new insights, and greater calm. This is when we begin to appreciate our potential for wisdom (albeit hard won) and growth, even under the most trying of circumstances.

Summary

Resiliency, meaning the strengths that we develop under trying, gut-wrenching circumstances, is finally receiving recognition as an important set of skills that we need to live a fulfilling life. It is the codependency antidote.

This is where the new "us" emerges: stronger, perhaps more humble—because we understand more about life's complexities; and certainly wiser—because we know ourselves so much better and are therefore much better equipped to handle the next challenge life is certain to throw at us.

And yes, we can be overwhelmed at times. But that doesn't mean we lose our skills; it just means we are having a setback. Our skills are still there waiting for us, and they will reemerge, probably enhanced by the experience.

Remember, a flower will always twist to the light. It may look straggly. It may grow between concrete blocks on a sidewalk. It may sprout up in a different location each year, moving to better light and moisture. But it will find nourishment. It will move to the light.

We are that flower. We can learn to persevere in whatever soil we are planted. We can learn to make needed changes and move to a better inner, and perhaps outer, location. This is our resilience in action.

CHAPTER 5

⌒

The Neurobiology
of Trauma

*Out of suffering have emerged
the strongest souls. . . .*

—EDWIN CHAPIN

We are all born with a mass of neurons (nerve cells). Establishing a working order for these neurons is one of the first tasks in our brain's development. The very young brain searches for order and meaning in earnest; later, we continue this task on a less intense level as adults. And the extent to which our brain can make sense of our environment will define our ability to have mastery over our lives.

This very early quest for order and meaning stimulates the brain to form networks of our neurons (neural pathways), literally linking them in a manner that allows us to make sense of what surrounds us. Our environment encourages the development of neuron connectivity. When we are infants (and continuing throughout our lifetime), we continually respond to our outside world and search for meaning. Smells, lights, sounds, temperature, and touch form our early infant environment.

Added to this is the infant's internal environment: feelings of hunger, thirst, discomfort, and a need to be held and soothed. In the beginning, all sensation is the same to an infant. And who dominates the infant's environment in the midst of all these sensations? Caregivers. And how we are cared for from birth begins a process that will continue throughout our lives: the process of connecting to our environment and mastering our surroundings so that we can survive, live, and hopefully thrive (Schore 1994).

Gradually, infants learn what is inside and what is outside of them. This leads to beginning to communicate with their caregivers more directly, often by crying differently. This very early form of communication is instinctively understood by those closest to the infant (Reyes and Elhai 2008). Caregivers are the first people with whom the infant connects. As such, they are powerful influences in shaping the developing brain.

Brain Growth: Efficiency in Action

Our brain seeks to be efficient from the beginning. When our brain responds to stimuli in the environment, it aligns our neurons accordingly by creating neural connections (chemical and electrical nerve mechanisms). These neural connections are templates, so to speak, that facilitate our responding in a more optimal way to the stimulus before us. And these complex and delicate chemical and electrical mechanisms form the basis of what becomes our intelligence and creativity.

Think of the brain as a very efficient organism. It is always searching for what it needs to survive and thrive. And what it doesn't need, it sheds, literally pruning itself. It rids itself of the excess neurons that are not required to form connections at a given moment. In fact, the brain operates on a very simple paradigm—use it or lose it! The brain does not keep what it does not need. This is one reason for having a rich array of positive stimulation in early childhood; it, in turn, stimulates the brain to grow and to develop.

The brain's pruning ability has certain benefits. For one, it gives the brain the flexibility that it needs to keep us alive and growing. The brain is very adaptable, particularly when we are young. As we get older, there is some truth in the adage, "You can't teach an old dog new tricks." As we age, our brain's ability to develop new neural pathways is more limited; however, it is still very possible to do this, and in fact we do this every day, even though at times it may feel like a s-t-r-e-t-c-h.

But the young brain is very pliable and it learns very quickly. And learning can be geometric and not linear. That is why at times we can see major jumps in a child's ability to, for example, learn to decode letters and read. The young brain is also very resilient. It can respond to an injury by having another area of the brain take over the affected area. And it can change rapidly as it responds to what is around it. Adaptability and resiliency ensure survival. When its self-pruning is complete, the brain is remarkably efficient. However, during a pruning period (in adolescence, for example), the brain does not function optimally.

How does the brain determine what it needs? It needs whatever is reinforced by the environment. And our environment becomes increasingly more complicated as we develop. We move from being dependent upon a primary caregiver to perhaps having multiple caregivers and other important figures and influences in our lives, including:

- **Who we live with:** Mother and father? Or a single mother and her boyfriend, or boyfriends? As an only child? As one of three siblings? Ten siblings? With a grandmother? With a grandmother as a primary caretaker? With a foster mother? Or multiple foster parents?
- **How we spend time:** Alone? With others? Playing alone with toys? Watching TV? Playing video games? Playing outdoors? Participating in group sports that teach cooperation, like soccer, baseball, or football? Solitary sports like track or horseback riding that focus on our personal best? Taking care of pets, which teaches us compassion and responsibility? Playing music or creating art, which fosters creativity?
- **Who we spend time with:** Immediate or large extended family, or both? Alone? With friends? And what type of friends are they? Supportive friends that we play with and use our imagination with? Bullies?
- **Where we spend time:** At home? In day care? In a safe environment? Or in one where we must be very careful of strangers? Gangs? Drug dealers? Cars? Supportive afterschool activities? In an organized religious setting? As part of a community?

Who teaches us, what entertains us, what is rewarded or punished in our actions, what threats and challenges are before us—all of these impact brain development. The environment is key in the shaping of the brain.

The Impact of Trauma

One important hallmark in the brain's self-pruning occurs around age ten. At that time, the brain is actively pruning, due not to what it needs on just a physiological level but also on a social level. Around age ten is when children begin to choose a value system based on what is good and useful for them to survive in the outside world.

A child who has been traumatized will inevitably incorporate and prioritize trauma survival in their brain. In this way, when life has been terribly unfair to a child, those traumas *physically change the brain*.

That means certain responses can be *hardwired*; that is, they become part of who the child, adolescent, and adult are due to the neural connections that have been developed and retained. This does not mean that the child can't learn additional ways of coping in the future to protect him- or herself, to react, and to learn new strategies that may be less stressful and less costly. Children can and do. It is important to remember that this trauma response is not all of whom the child is and will become, but it is an important part, and for very good reason (Schore 1994).

How the Brain Reacts to Trauma

As hard as some of us have tried to deal with trauma, not every attempt has been successful. Sometimes we feel thwarted, undermined by ourselves. As the brain develops (and especially during periods of pruning), it is very vulnerable to stress, which is why, for example, in emotionally charged situations, teens often overreact. But as adults, we have a different set of standards for ourselves. We can be very hard on ourselves, which is why it is important to have a basic understanding of how trauma operates. With that knowledge, we can begin to forgive ourselves for being so very reactive, and we also can try to heal. As our brains develop, we also produce ways of mediating and controlling some of our earlier neural pathways. This is controlled by actual structures in the brain, as we will discuss shortly (Lanius, Vermetten, and Pain 2010).

Triggers

When triggered, we may literally act like a two-year-old. We may have a tantrum, scream, hit, or want to throw ourselves on the ground. This is because what has been triggered is the neural pathway that we developed at an earlier age. For that reason we may feel like a *time traveler,* moving back and forth between then and now. With trauma survivors, this movement is often rapid and without warning.

Not all triggers are unpleasant. When we hear a song from our youth, we may feel a rush of sexual excitement as we are transported back to the backseat of that car where we lost our virginity, even if we are now eighty. Or we might feel a rush of memories on a crisp fall day as we are transported back to our youth by the smell of the leaves and the feel of the sun.

Psychologist Peter Levine (2010) speaks about triggers in terms of energy and the ability of a threat to literally overwhelm the activating systems of the brain. Here, if the energy from the threat is not discharged successfully, the actual moment that the threat occurred, along with its accompanying feelings and behaviors, becomes imprinted in the brain. And each time this moment of threat is revisited by the body and the brain through being triggered, and each time the perceived threat is responded to—first biochemically and then behaviorally with actions designed to minimize this threat—a "blueprint" of attempted survival strategies is created and stored in both the body and the brain. For this reason, it is important to embrace the notion that we each do our best to survive, even when we feel that we are in the process of being overwhelmed. Each response is stored in the body and in the brain and becomes part of our response repertoire to be used the next time. So change is not as easy as saying "I'll do it differently," because our responses become wired in.

With high arousal, our *sympathetic* nervous system becomes activated. We go on elevated alert; we move into high gear. The sympathetic nervous system is the brain's gas pedal, its accelerator. We become ready for action: our breath gets shallow, our pupils become enlarged, our heart rate increases, our mouth becomes dry. We then move to activate our *parasympathetic* nervous system, our internal brake, and as we try to calm down, our heart rate slows, we breathe more normally, and we're able to swallow again. Each system attempts to balance the other (Siegel 1999).

Trauma Affects Bonding

How a child bonds with his or her caregiver is complicated if the caregiver is responsible for the child being traumatized. Experiencing trauma may cause the child to withdraw and be less responsive to the caregiver or try to avoid the caregiver. And the infant or child may generalize this response to other caregivers, resulting in the child not actively learning from his environment as he seeks to protect himself. Once the child's brain begins to expect not to be cared for, or it is triggered by the actions of the caregiver or the environment, bonding will most likely be adversely affected.

It is difficult for an infant or child to understand why he or she isn't being cared for. The caregiver's unavailability due to illness, depression, or substance use matters little and feels much the same to the child if nurturing is lacking. The child's behaviors will follow accordingly, perhaps dramatically influencing the caregiver, who in turn will react to the child (Schore 1994). Problems with attachment can lead to the development of *shame* and *dissociation* (Fogash and Copeley 2008), and to the adaptation to this that we have been addressing throughout the book—codependency.

How the Brain Functions

To understand how we make these adaptations, we must understand how our brain functions. The brain develops in segments from back to front. The brain stem is the *survival brain*, the oldest part of the brain from an evolutionary standpoint. This regulates our basic body functions like body temperature, breathing, and heart rate.

The next function to develop is the limbic system, or the *emotional brain*, crucial in how we react to trauma. The limbic system is the emotional core of the brain and is involved in the creation and experience of emotion and memory. The limbic system is made of several brain structures. Those that play a prominent role when trauma is experienced or re-experienced through being triggered are the *amygdala*, *hippocampus*, *hypothalamus*, and *thalamus*.

The amygdala is the structure responsible for integrating emotional reactions to both pleasurable and adverse experiences. It also is responsible for determining which memories are stored and where they are stored in the brain. The amygdala responds to a variety of emotional stimuli but mostly those related to fear and anxiety. As such, it is our *threat-sensitive* indicator. When we are triggered due to trauma, this is a part of our brain that is activated. The amygdala and its central nucleus communicate with many brain regions including those that control breathing, motor function, autonomic (involuntary) response, and hormone release, as well as the processing of internal and external information.

When activated, the amygdala sends a stress hormone to the hippocampus. Part of the hippocampus's function is to store actual memories so that they are available long term; it also retrieves those memories. However, if the stress hormone levels released by the amygdala are high enough, they can impede this function of the hippocampus, either by causing it to have problems taking in a recent memory and storing it efficiently, or in retrieving a memory. This is why we can have fragments of memories and even remember feelings, body sensations, and smells, but we can't remember the events associated with them. These traumatic memory fragments tend to be sensory and are difficult to retrieve; they are also more difficult to describe using language than are other memories.

The hypothalamus is an important emotional center that controls the feelings of exhilaration, anger, and unhappiness. It also plays a role in the panic caused when one is triggered by increasing the anxiety experienced. The hypothalamus facilitates behaviors such as pleasure, rage, aversion, displeasure, and uncontrollably loud laughter.

The thalamus processes and relays movement and sensory information. It is essentially a relay station that takes in sensory information and then passes it on to the *cerebral cortex*, the *thinking* part of the brain.

The cerebral cortex forms an outer covering around the brain that accounts for 85 percent of the human brain mass. The cortex is where reason, logic, and rational thinking originate. This is where we try to process our trauma rationally; as we know, rational processing has its limitations as a sole strategy to use in dealing with trauma (Liberzon et al. 1999).

The Brain, Trauma, and the Exacerbating Role of Alcohol and Drugs

Alcohol and other drugs tend to be dis-inhibitors. That means they reduce our ability to control our physical and emotional responses. When someone picks up a beer or a glass of wine to unwind, to relax, or to float away, it is to reach out to a part of the brain that isn't thinking as much and isn't as worried.

The problem here is that for the person with a trauma background, this floating or moving away from the dominance of the cortex (the thinking brain) to the more emotional part of the brain can be fraught with danger if he or she is triggered. It means that if there is something potentially triggering in the environment—a smell, a look, a conversation—the person with a trauma history may have just a little less ability to manage the trigger responses when under the influence of alcohol or drugs.

This decreased ability, as slight as it may be, can make all the difference between being triggered or not. And if the person is triggered, alcohol and/or drug use can make the difference in the degree to which they are triggered and how quickly they can rebound. If someone is already under the influence of alcohol and/or drugs, once he is triggered, the response will be more extreme, more upsetting than it would have been because he will not be in as much control. As a consequence, he will have less ability to remember to use his coping skills than if they weren't compromised biochemically (NIAAA 2011; Evans and Sullivan 1995). This is seen clearly in the following statistics:

- 25–75 percent of survivors of abusive or violent trauma report problematic alcohol use.

- 10–33 percent of survivors of accident, illness, or disaster trauma report problematic alcohol use, especially if troubled by persistent health problems or pain.
- Being diagnosed with PTSD increases the risk of developing an alcohol use disorder.
- Veterans over the age of 65 with PTSD are at increased risk for attempted suicide if they experience problematic alcohol use or depression (VA National Center for PTSD 2011).
- Recent epidemiological studies suggest that as many as half of all veterans diagnosed with PTSD also have a co-occurring substance use disorder (NIDA 2012).
- Alcohol consumption is used by both men and women as a way to cope with childhood sexual abuse (Miller et al. 1997).

Making a decision as to whether or not to use alcohol and drugs, under what circumstances, and to what extent will always remain a personal decision. All we can advise is that this decision be carefully considered and the determination be made, at least in part, by how high your stress level is, how relaxing your environment is, and what triggers are potentially there. And remember, even considering all this may not be enough to ward off a traumatic reaction.

Summary

Our brain is a remarkable organ. It has the ability to grow in a planned and artful manner. It is flexible, malleable, and highly responsive to our environment. If our environment is rich with trauma, then this will influence how the brain learns to organize itself, how it lays down memory, and the quality of these memories when we later try to retrieve them. Our brain has several sections that all work together to produce the self that we know. Our survival brain communicates with our emotional brain, and lastly communicates with our thinking brain. All parts of our brain are involved in any traumatic response that we have. And all of the parts of our brain are affected by alcohol and drug use, which compromises our ability to manage potential triggers.

❧

CHAPTER 6

The Principles of Healing Trauma and Codependency

Believe that life is worth living and your belief will help create the fact.

—WILLIAM JAMES

B elieving that we can get better, that we can recover, is an important first step in the healing process, even though less is understood about how the brain heals than about how it responds to trauma. We do know that the brain continues to modify its neural pathways throughout our life. This is an organic response to our environment. The way we change our environment, and more importantly, the way we change our behavior, can begin to alter the pathways in our brain. Those who are focused on this aspect of neurobiology—the emerging understanding of healing—stress the importance of the development of new, novel experiences that will stimulate the brain to grow in new directions—to literally make new connections. The reparative and restorative experiences described in this book are key tools for making these new connections.

The Twelve Principles of Healing

The process of healing is best understood when it is looked at as a process composed of twelve principles:

One: Healing Takes Time

Let's face it, most of us did not get here overnight, and we won't leave here overnight. In fact, if we could, it would be overwhelming in and of itself, so that's not really a goal. Given this, we need to learn to determine a pace at which we can process what we are feeling, and we need to understand why we are feeling it. And as we do this, we need to learn how to manage our trauma triggers and our codependent urges, even as more triggers and our response—codependency—are stirred up.

Yes, it is quite a task, but what alternative do we have? Do we want to continue to feel as we do? We can choose to do that . . . or we can begin to resolve what is going on within us by pacing ourselves, not getting discouraged, treating this as a journey and not as a destination, and knowing that we can take a break when it feels like too much. As we begin to take the pressure off and realize that this healing takes time, we find that we begin to feel the freedom that comes with not burdening ourselves to *rush into wellness*. We begin to feel better. This is one of the paradoxes of healing from trauma.

Two: Healing Is Not Linear

Much as we would like to go from points A to B to C, healing doesn't work like that. Not for a skinned knee, and certainly not for trauma. We heal in ways that make sense to our neural connectors. And we heal in ways that make sense to us emotionally, both verbally and (perhaps most important) nonverbally. And healing is not uniform. We'll have setbacks, which we hope will become spaced increasingly farther apart over time. But they will occur. It's all part of the process. So we might as well put on our "curious hat" and become an active participant: see what works and what doesn't work, at least for now. Be open to other options. Stay engaged and chart the course of our treatment by actively taking care of ourselves, by actively self-parenting, as we remain amazed and grateful for what we find actually works.

Three: The Mind and Body Act as One

Researchers Elizabeth Osuch and Charles Engel (2004) emphasize the very strong correlation between mind and body, with a focus on how changing the body can change the mind and, as we now know, the neural circuits. One way to do this is through yoga (see Appendix, page 228). In yoga, the rhythmic deep breathing not only slows the thinking brain but also our physical responses. Heart rate and thinking slow down; inner organs are massaged, cleansing the lymph system, kidneys, lungs, skin, and digestive and elimination organs. All this leads to a greater sense of well-being.

Four: Reparative, Restorative, Self-Soothing Experiences Are Key

Noted trauma expert Bessel A. van der Kolk, M.D., emphasizes that insight alone is not sufficient to promote healing (2003). Yes, it is a component of healing; it is important to understand what happened, how we felt then, how it makes us feel now, and what triggers us into remembering. But this is not enough. Van der Kolk urges the development of *reparative experiences* that can directly contradict the learned helplessness and the psychic freezing that accompany most traumas. This is literally a clarion call to action for all of us. We offer reparative and restorative self-soothing exercises in Part Two.

Five: Changing Your Actions Changes Your Thinking

This axiom is one of the many paradoxes involved in the process of healing. We often think of this principle the other way around—that we must first understand something before we can change it. But that is not always the case. A truism that many of us have grown up with is: "Fake it till your make it!" This slogan has found its way into many situations and is a favorite learned by those who enter such programs as Alcoholics Anonymous and Al-Anon. It quite simply speaks to the power that changing our actions can have on not only our thinking but also our sense of well-being. When combined with *redefining time* (which we will look at in a moment) this principle also speaks to the power of desire combined with will—and lots of social support, such as AA and Al-Anon meetings, self-parenting retreats, and other healing actions we can take to change well-ingrained behaviors, and biochemical triggers.

Six: Allow Rather than Force

We can learn to allow something to happen the way it is meant to happen rather than force it to be a certain way—even if we know that "allowing" is going to hurt. When we develop experience in managing traumatic and codependent responses, we learn that we do indeed have power. We cannot control what enters our mind. We can control how long it stays there—by anticipating the trigger and preparing for how we will manage it. Anticipation and preparation help to normalize our response to a trigger, and thus we gain some measure of control over it.

We assert control by not trying to be in control, and this is another paradox of healing. Once we are startled or triggered, we can decide that we do not have to go full tilt by overreacting. When our mind races, busily making connections and creating horrors in our head, we can take control by *allowing* the thought but not indulging it. Or we can work to eliminate the thought as we will show you how to do in Part Two. We can witness our pain but still hold it outside of ourselves so it is not felt again with the same intensity; we have the power to keep it from igniting our latent trauma. (We'll also discuss this more in Part Two.) But for right now, know that this process of "allowing, not forcing" is ongoing and produces results.

Seven: Own the Power of Our Nonverbal Communications

Actions do speak louder than words. Sometimes we become caught by the need to articulate, respond verbally, or write. These strategies are important, but they only encompass part of our brain. We have vast abilities to process feelings, traumas, and other experiences nonverbally. And when we use both the verbal and nonverbal parts of our brains, we increase our potential to move forward.

Some scientists argue that nonverbal strategies—including engaging in any of the creative arts—may have more power than merely verbal ones because they involve the parts of the brain that were engaged during our experience of trauma—the senses (Osuch and Engel 2004). Other parts of the brain assist us, including the *nucleus accumbens*, which directs motivated behavior. This part of our brain is responsible for how much effort we expend to seek rewards and is part of the pleasure center of the brain. We can make healing pleasurable!

The healing potential of creative art is just beginning to be under-stood. Dance and movement; sketching and painting; sculpture; writing poetry, short stories, and novels; journaling; and music are all ways that we can heal using verbal and nonverbal means. Novel-ist Stephen King, painter Frida Kahlo, and composer Peter Ilyich Tchaikovsky are all trauma survivors—thrivers—who used their art as a way of repairing after traumatic experiences.

Conferences in California and Canada have been devoted to exploring art as a healing paradigm for more than ten years, and in 2012, the conservative New York State Psychological Convention will be fully devoted to exploring the arts and healing. This is where the cutting edge of the neurobiology of healing is heading.

Eight: Embrace DEF—Diet, Exercise, Fun

We are biochemical beings. As such, we are incredibly sensitive to what we put into our bodies, how we feed ourselves. It is important that we follow dietary guidelines that make sense for our individual circumstances. Whether you are a vegan or a carnivore, you need to make sure that you follow a balanced diet to ensure that you receive the right nutrients. What we recommend is that when cooking for yourself, you imagine serving your meal to someone else, and ask yourself if it is healthy.

We also need to respect how we treat our bodies. This can be difficult for many with codependency because so much energy is directed toward taking care of others; finding time for self-care can be a challenge. So be creative about how you exercise. Have a set of weights by your television or your reading chair and use them. Walk the stairs instead of taking the elevator; exercise, stretch, and protect your body, knowing that as you do this you are also releas-ing tension.

And learn to have fun again. Spend some creative energy considering what is fun for you: watching a game with friends, baking, walking, playing tennis or golf, listening to music, doing yoga, or meditating. Remember that we all need re-creation time, time to allow us to integrate our experiences and come at them in a new way.

Nine: It's Good to Slow Time

A radio commentator on the National Public Radio (NPR) affiliate WAMC in Albany, New York, uses a method he calls "the slowing of time" when soliciting donations for a matching pledge. As the allotted time is about to expire, he "slows time" so that all the new donations will count and qualify for the increase in money represented by the matching pledge. This is done with great drama and fanfare: his speech slows, his voice deepens, and his breathing becomes heavy. This technique of "slowing time" has a direct application when dealing with trauma.

When we begin to deal with our trauma triggers, it is not unusual to find that we may need to slow down our responses every day or even several times a day. This can be very challenging, but it can be rewarding, too, because you will find that learning how to slow time puts you in charge of your life. When we are able to literally take control of time, we begin to experience some relief.

We all practice some form of slowing time: we've learned to count to ten, leave the room, bite our tongue, walk away and regroup, refrain from sending an e-mail, text, or tweet in anger. Dealing with trauma triggers and codependency urges are no different. We can begin to slow down our reactions. We can also turn to established programs like AA and Al-Anon. They have some core strategies that will help us, including another slogan: "One day at a time." Yes, just take care of today! Another way of thinking about this is "just stay in the present."

There are many holistic approaches that also serve to slow time and begin the healing process. These include meditation, mindfulness, spiritual disciplines (including prayer), dance, and the arts (Osuch and Engel 2004). In *Train Your Mind, Change Your Brain* (2007), for example, author Sharon Begley writes about the importance of mindfulness in teaching people that they are *not* their thoughts or their fears or their flashbacks. Embracing this concept frees individuals to see those thoughts, fears, or flashbacks as a separate part of who they are, a part that may require attention but does not comprise their full identity.

Neuropsychiatrist Daniel Siegel (2007) elaborates on the difference between the narrative mind that plans and worries, and the sensing mind that experiences what is around us. He stresses the importance of being aware of our senses as a means of slowing and changing our thinking. Here the focus is developing an awareness of our senses: what touches our skin; what we smell, hear, or see; how different parts of our body feel. And this awareness becomes a means of anchoring us in the moment and away from worrying or intrusive thoughts.

Another excellent time-slowing strategy that really works is meditation (Ritskes et al. 2003). Meditation can blunt the immediacy of the trauma trigger by creating another space to be in, one we have developed, one in which we have control. Here, by slowing the breath, we slow our responses. By focusing only on our breath, or on nothing, we slow our thinking. By slowing our thinking and our responses, we are able to control our triggers.

Another set of strategies involves slowing how we move; for example, driving a couple of miles under the speed limit can be a way of taking control. Other ways are walking more slowly with greater purpose, moving with more measured gestures, and speaking more slowly—all to gain control of our responses to the situation before us.

All these strategies help us focus on being in the present and can provide incredible relief as we form new behaviors and new neural pathways to deal with existing stresses and triggers. Focusing on the present allows us to use other neural pathways we might have developed for other purposes—such as dealing with our boss or our children—to instead address what is triggering us.

Ten: We Can Give Our Trauma Away

Spiritual practices can have profound effects on us, particularly in releasing us from the aloneness of dealing with our trauma and codependency. We can *turn over* our experience—our will and mind—to a *higher power* (our Higher Parent, the Universe, our God), even in the face of great challenges. We see this in prayers from different faiths, where the people presenting petitions add, "Thy will be done" and in that instance *turn over* their needs to their spiritual guide. In the Jewish, Christian, and Islamic traditions, this practice is repeated in the psalms: "Cast your cares on the LORD and he will sustain you; he will never let the righteous fall" (Psalm 55:22). The turning over of one's worries to a higher power, and believing that this force will support you in dealing with them, is a profound decision, one that can be life-altering, and one that is *only* ours to make.

When we do this in moments of great challenge, we may experience a release, a distancing from our stress and our trauma, perhaps even a feeling of calm. Through connecting to our Higher Power, our God, or our Higher Parent, we create a space, an inner oasis, where we can connect to our inner self, our spiritual self, while also letting in outside support.

We can take control by releasing ourselves from the need to be alone with the terrible events that have so shaped our lives. And in giving our trauma and codependency over to a higher power, we clear our minds by *not* requiring immediate results. At that point, our worries are in some other being's hands or in the hands of the Universe, and we can take a deep breath and begin to let go of our concern. This is another paradox of healing: only we can do it, but we cannot do it alone.

Eleven: Sometimes We Need a Pharmacological Assist

Yes, a "pharmacological assist" means medication. Sometimes, no matter how hard we try, no matter how committed we are, no matter how many therapists we see, no matter how many different approaches we try or meetings we attend, we do not successfully control our trauma enough to have the life we would like. We try and try, and we make progress, but sometimes we cannot do this alone.

There is often great shame attached to using medication, as if it is our fault that we need something external to our body to assist in controlling our triggers. Indeed, we have found this is a common response from people who tried to self-medicate by using alcohol and drugs. It is interesting that in our healing, our shame can so dominate an important decision that we may refuse to consider what could be the last piece of the puzzle in our recovery.

Feeling that we have to do it alone is our *compulsive self-reliance* in action. We do not have to do it alone. We can effectively challenge this part of our codependency by taking the medical action that is recommended to us. And taking a prescribed medication will be much more effective than trying to determine what to take on our own. Whether this be a mood stabilizer, an atypical antipsychotic being prescribed to control our anxiety, an antidepressant, or an antianxiety medication—or more than one medication—each can provide a powerful measure of pharmacological control, important when we are not able to do this on our own.

Remember, our neural receptors are electrical and biochemical. Sometimes we are lacking in the amount of biochemicals we need to feel the way we would like to feel. Due to heredity, the extreme stress of multiple traumas, and perhaps significant alcohol or drug use, our brains may not be working at an ideal level to produce a sense of well-being. Medication can assist in providing this; it can be of invaluable assistance in reducing the severity of triggers and the nightmares associated with trauma. For some, having the courage to agree to be evaluated to see if medication could help is a major step in the self-parenting process, which we'll cover in more detail in Part Two.

Twelve: Don't Take It Personally

As we begin to change how we see and approach others, we will be met with a range of reactions from people. Some reactions are positive, and people are supportive of our growth, our change, our recovery. But other reactions may not be positive. People may need to take some time to process the changes they see in us; they may be surprised or even threatened by the differences they see. Don't take this personally. Other people's reactions are mostly about themselves, their history, and their needs. We are not responsible for others; that is our codependency in action. Remember, it is enough to be responsible for ourselves. As Don Miguel Ruiz states in his epic book *The Four Agreements* (1997), when we take personally the actions or attitudes of others, it is akin to letting their poison-tipped daggers stab at our heart. We need to protect our hearts and ourselves, and allow the actions of others to be about them, not about us.

Summary:

The neurobiology of healing from trauma is an emerging field. We know less about healing than we do about the actual mechanisms for storing and retrieving traumatic material. But the neurobiology of healing is alive, growing well, and beginning to attract more mainstream researchers as those impacted by trauma, those who love them, and clinicians clamor for some hard data. What is emerging is a picture of common principles that enhance healing from trauma, elements that are available for individual use and can be combined into our personal recovery plan as we learn to self-parent.

Serenity Prayer

*God, grant me the serenity to accept
the things I cannot change,
the courage to change the things I can,
and the wisdom to know the difference.*

—REINHOLD NIEBUHR

Part Two:

The Self-Parenting Process

Self-parenting is about guiding yourself through a process that allows you to become who you would like to be—who you were meant to be—by healing yourself through self-nurturing. How well you learn to self-parent determines how well you go through life.

In this second half of the book, you will be given specific directions for self-parenting, including exercises and meditations to help you begin the self-parenting process. You'll be encouraged to journal as a way to learn to live mindfully, a way to know what you are thinking, and a way to implant new ideas into your subconscious mind. All the exercises are designed to give you new tools for self-nurturing. As you start to chart your self-parenting journey, a plan of action will emerge that will give you a clear path to recovery!

CHAPTER 7

❧

STEP ONE:

We Admitted We Have Been Traumatized and We Are Codependent

*The greatest discovery of any generation
is that a human being can alter his
life by altering his attitude.*

—WILLIAM JAMES

*J*ane *felt like she had nowhere to turn. Her life just wasn't working. Even though she had a well-paying job as an emergency room
nurse, she felt empty. Her relationship with Tim, her fiancé, was falling apart, and she didn't know why. On the surface, Jane thought they
had a good relationship. But she felt that she worked twice as hard as
he did in the relationship, and she resented the fact that he wasn't as
invested in it as she was. The reality was, as Jane was to find out later,*

her compulsive self-reliance didn't allow Tim much room for being a real partner. Another problem was that Jane didn't trust Tim, and he knew that and couldn't understand why, as he'd never given her reason not to.

Jane knew that her lack of trust was due to her childhood traumas. She had been sexually abused by a neighbor when she was seven. Years later, she'd witnessed a fatal car accident that left her with nightmares. And her job in the emergency room was constantly triggering her previous traumas. She didn't understand that her coping strategy of codependency was interfering with her relationship with Tim and was keeping her from feeling fulfilled.

Jane is a victim of complex trauma. Her life is a mess, but she doesn't know why. She understands that the sexual abuse traumatized her. But she isn't aware that the combination of the sexual abuse, the car accident, and the constant trauma in the ER are impacting her in every area of her life.

Recognizing Codependency

Our first step to change is admitting we have a problem; this is a major issue for trauma survivors and codependents. Denial is a primary defense mechanism for victims of trauma and children of addicts. We deny because to admit and feel the full impact of our past is to feel the depth of our pain and fear. This is not something we ever look forward to feeling.

We are invested in looking good and being in control, and we often deny our problems. How could we have problems when so many people we know look to us to help them with their lives? Yet the truth is that we *do* need help, and in many ways our lives *are* out of control.

All too often, trauma survivors who are codependents wait until they are in crisis or suffer severe loss to change their self-defeating behaviors. Similar to alcoholics, trauma survivors and codependents have to hit bottom and become desperate before they seek help.

Step One identifies the need to admit that bad things happened to us. We do not let that fact defeat us, and in fact, when we admit what happened, we begin the process of mastering our trauma. We surrender to the reality of our past, but we in no way admit defeat. When we surrender, we actually win; in a sense, we win by understanding the nature of our loss.

This admission may also include recognizing that we need to change our relationships in fundamental ways. This may mean letting go of people in our lives who we once thought we could not live without—including friends, coworkers, and maybe even parents, spouses, or significant others. We need to let some go to make room for new relationships.

The Illusion of Control

For a trauma survivor who is also a codependent, life is often all about regaining control. The lives of codependents and trauma survivors are based on maintaining control because the loss of control implies chaos and a lack of safety on a very basic level. Control is the illusion of safety and protection that allows trauma survivors to live each day without the terror they felt when they were first exposed to trauma. Control is the armor survivors wear to help maintain the illusion that they are safe from harm and will not be hurt again.

Of course, the belief that we can maintain total control is a fallacy. Bad things happen regardless of what we do. We cannot always protect those we love, or even ourselves. We cannot stop bad things from happening. But we can control how we respond when bad things do happen, and we can control the meaning we give to those events. We can see others and ourselves as heroic individuals who have survived and even thrived, regardless of the circumstance of our lives. We can give ourselves credit for the many ways we have learned to self-parent when bad things happened.

The Benefit of Self-Parenting

When we surrender to the reality of our past and admit the unmanageability caused by our trauma and codependency, we embrace our past with compassion. When we admit we have a problem and we let our higher self be in charge, we allow a greater consciousness and spiritual connection to take over; we truly learn how to self-parent. This spiritual connection will come into play again in the coming steps, but the door to a higher power is opened in Step One.

Step One allows us to reap the rewards of humility. When we are willing to surrender to the reality of our past, we leave behind arrogance and self-will and allow grace to enter our lives. When we admit that we have reached our bottom, we are through with the pain that we have caused ourselves by relying only on ourselves to fix our lives. Step One allows us to truly surrender to our reality and stop hiding from our past.

Identifying the Impact of Unresolved Trauma

How do we begin? We start by identifying the impact that unresolved trauma is having on us. We examine ourselves to see if the symptoms of trauma explained in the earlier chapters apply to us.

Chapter 1 includes a comprehensive list of trauma symptoms. Please reread that list on pages 23 through 26 and see how many you identify with. Remember, after a lifetime of coping, it is hard to admit that we have failed to master our problems effectively. Our coping strategies have sometimes failed us and left us exhausted and clueless about how to heal ourselves. Only by admitting the full extent of the impact of our past trauma can we find new ways of healing. Step One is about admitting the problem and then letting go of it so we can heal!

Self-Parenting for Healing

When we let go and admit we need help, we can begin to gain perspective on our problems and finally have a real chance to heal. When we are standing too close to our problems, we cannot see them for what they are. Unfortunately, many of us think that if we see our problems for what they are, we will become overwhelmed. It is imperative to change the way we think about life if we are to become all that we are meant to be. Trauma keeps us from this because it creates fear and negative expectation.

When we self-parent, we learn to counter fear with faith and change our thinking by letting go and admitting that the old ways do not work anymore. We admit we need help and begin anew. When we change the way we see ourselves, we learn to define ourselves by the positive experiences in our lives instead of the negative ones. We let go of an old identity that is based on a negative experience and learn to start anew as a free and different person. *We begin to live our life instead of our story!* When we live our story of trauma and codependency, we keep reenforcing destructive thoughts in our consciousness and creating a world full of negative expectations. When we learn to self-parent, we give voice to a greater part of ourselves that knows we have to admit our fears and then let go of the past to move to a new future.

Charting Your Recovery

In each of the twelve steps that make up this section of the book, you'll find exercises and journaling prompts to guide you on your healing journey. Each chapter will become part of a chart for your recovery. Like any chart, this one will be a map to guide you in creating a new life, one without fear and toxic behaviors. This chart of affirmations, meditations, and soul exercises will give you a personalized blueprint for a compelling future. It will be helpful for you to keep a small notebook with you to keep track of affirmations or self-soothing exercises that may occur to you. Create subsections entitled My Affirmations, My Self-Soothing Exercises, My Codependency Connections, and My Journal. You will develop a "Recovery Plan" by adding your personal healing ideas to the ones supplied in this book.

Let the Healing Begin

Self-Parenting Affirmations

I am whole and complete,
and I can only get better and better.

I build on my strengths,
and I eliminate my weaknesses.

I am, without a doubt,
the best me I can be.

 ## Self-Soothing Exercises that Repair and Restore: Staying Grounded

It is very important to stay grounded during your recovery process. As you begin self-parenting work, if you are feeling disoriented, confused, or upset you can do the following exercise:

- Sit on a chair or a comfortable piece of furniture. Feel your feet on the ground, connecting to Mother Earth. Press your hands on your thighs. Be aware of the seat and feel your back against the chair.

- Look around you and pick six objects that have red or blue in them. This should allow you to feel in the present, more grounded, and in your body. Notice how your breath gets deeper and calmer.

- You may want to go outdoors and find a peaceful place to sit on the grass, among the falling leaves, or in the snow. Feel how your body can be held and supported by the ground.

- Notice the ability of the earth to support you as you
  focus on what is ahead of you (Ross and Levine, 2011).

 ## Codependency Connection

Codependency is an outgrowth of a dysfunctional home. Where there is trauma, there is usually a disruption in family functioning. We begin to overcompensate for our trauma by overfunctioning or becoming hypervigilant. In either case, we lose sight of what we need to do for ourselves, and we lose track of our own needs. When we become healthy, we learn to put our needs first. We recognize that if we are not well, we cannot help others effectively, and that is the first step on the road to recovery.

 ## My Journal

As part of your Step One journal, write about the incidents from childhood that were traumatizing to you. These can be incidents of traumatic events or generalized feelings that left you feeling frightened and alone. Also describe ways your family functioned that left you feeling confused and unsafe. Remember we are charting incidents in your life that caused trauma and started you on the road to codependency!

CHAPTER 8

∾

STEP TWO:

We Asked for Spiritual Help and Let Go of Compulsive Self-Reliance

What is needed is to learn afresh,
to observe, and to discover for ourselves,
the meaning of wholeness.

—DAVID BOHM, *WHOLENESS AND THE IMPLICATE ORDER*

*R*on was highly intelligent and very self-sufficient, and he had always prided himself on his ability to work through any problem. Lately though, he couldn't figure out how to heal his life, how to move on, how to break out of despair.

His father had been an alcoholic for as long as Ron could remember. Ron was the responsible one in his family. He was his mother's confidant and her helper. He had been a good athlete and an A student. He *was self-reliant to a fault: he needed help from no one, and he prided himself on his independence.*

Ron joined the Marine Corps when he was twenty-one. He had a rigorous boot camp experience, as all Marines do. But he was grateful for that experience; he felt he had learned how to "man up" in boot camp. He was confident that his training had prepared him for combat, but that proved wrong when he was deployed to Iraq.

He was assigned to a medical unit that picked up wounded soldiers and flew them to field hospitals. He was constantly ministering to soldiers who had been horribly maimed. He witnessed dying soldiers who screamed for their mothers, men begging to die because their pain was so great. He saw men lose their arms and legs. He felt helpless to ease their suffering, and he became ashamed that he himself was whole.

Ron's trauma hung over his head like a cloud of sadness, always lurking somewhere in his consciousness; it was a ghost that haunted him whenever he felt happy. He felt he was in some way dishonoring the memory of those he had cared for if he enjoyed himself. His lack of joy undermined his life in all aspects.

Ron finally sought help from a therapist when he began to contemplate suicide. During therapy, Ron was able to realize that he did not believe he could change his life. He did not believe he could find peace. His journey to recovery began with his fight to let go of his guilt and the total self-reliance that was no longer working for him.

Origins of Compulsive Self-Reliance

Like Ron, all of us who have experienced trauma have learned to rely on ourselves and little else. We've become experts in compulsive self-reliance. Out of necessity, our natural gifts—our intelligence, resourcefulness, and persistence—were used to keep our families and us safe. However, this strategy left us like Ron: isolated and desperate.

Those who suffered trauma learned over time to take over every situation and solve every problem presented. While this sense of responsibility is exhausting, it is also rewarding. Competence feels good. If children feel competent, they tend to have elevated self-esteem, so children of trauma often compensate by becoming overly competent.

Remember yourself as a child, and you will probably identify with some of these traits. Resilient children are likeable and often leaders. But they are also often "parentified children." They are victims of parental role reversal in which they end up taking care of their parents even though they are children, which can lead to many dysfunctional behaviors. Parentified children have a high risk for depression. They also have a high tolerance for codependent relationships and are usually compulsive caregivers. They have a low tolerance for separation, which helps us to understand why they stay in bad relationships for so long. Perhaps the most telling characteristic of parentified children is the overwhelming number of them who choose the helping professions as their career.

Our compulsive self-reliance and our resilience have been useful, but they have also left us alone in a desert of our own design. We have learned to live in isolation. This dependence on self replaces dependence on others or a higher power. To move beyond relying only on ourselves, we must have faith in something greater.

Letting Go of Compulsive Self-Reliance

Compulsive self-reliance has been our curse and our savior. We have learned from childhood that dependence on self is best. After years of disappointment in our families, we become a family unto ourselves. We become successful in all things save one: feeling safe and loved. We do not allow for failure, even when it is apparent that we have failed. We compulsively try to fix others and fail to fix ourselves. We focus on others and fail to see what we need for ourselves.

We have been applauded for our intellect, which has been our best friend and has saved us in chaotic situations. In the end though, relying on our intellect leaves us in a world where dependence on self is everything. When we move beyond intellect and let faith in, something greater takes over. We move into a new dimension of meaning and spiritual growth that takes us beyond our experience into a world of wholeness, serenity, and love. This new experience is based in present life instead of on our past trauma.

As a young adult, Ron looked to the military to give his life meaning, and for a while it did. However, because of his sense of responsibility and his compassion, he was left empty. He did his best to save those he could, and he exhausted himself in the process. Jake, the returning veteran we met in Chapter 1, followed the same path. And while their caretaking or codependence was in many ways heroic, both Ron and Jake found themselves looking for help.

As codependents who have experienced trauma, we end up in the same relationships, picking the same self-centered or abusive mates, and we end up repeating the pain of the past. We re-create the pain of our childhood and then wonder how we could end up in pain and confusion again. We wind up in jobs that demand everything from us but offer little in return. It is as though we live in an endless cycle of repeated trauma that we can't seem to break.

Many of us find ourselves living in isolation, alone with our trauma or childhood pain. We end up alone in a totally controlled self-imposed prison of solitary confinement, and we forget that we have the key to set ourselves free. That key is our higher power! Letting go is the only way to move beyond our compulsive self-reliance. We take the leap into faith when we finally let Step Two work in our lives.

Believing in Someone or Something Greater than Ourselves

Our higher power is our path to true empowerment. In believing in the possibility of a higher power, we find a source for change greater than any we have experienced before. Knowing that this power is an aspect of ourselves that is available to us at any time creates for the first time a true sense of safety, a source of protection that is with us always.

As we move from the tyranny of self-reliance, we become a member of the human community. We open the door to faith and new possibilities of hope. We are no longer alone, because our higher power is with us everywhere we go and exists as a resource we can always call on.

Faith implies hope. Trauma survivors and codependents often lack hope. They feel they have been abandoned by God, and with good reason. After all, what kind of god would let the terrible things that they have experienced happen? Our belief is that if we rely on ourselves, we cannot be betrayed. We believe on some level that God betrayed us, and we will never make the mistake of trusting in God again. So out of fear of betrayal and disappointment, we don't allow ourselves to ask for help from God. We have been trained to believe that help is not a possibility for us. All too often, help was not available when we needed it in our lives before, so why should we expect help to be available now?

Remember, we live in the world we believe exists. If we believe the world is full of untrustworthy people with whom we need to be cautious, we will find those people in our lives. Moving from reliance on self to reliance on God is *huge*. We need an open mind to make that leap of faith. We need to nurture honesty, open-mindedness, and willingness. When we open ourselves to a new view of life, we open the door to new possibilities.

The second step gives us hope—hope for a life full of safety, love, comfort, and abundance! And along with the hope we derive from working Step Two, we find that our way of thinking is undergoing a radical change. The whole world looks different. We open ourselves to new ideas. We step away from the problem and toward a spiritual solution.

Self-Parenting for Healing

By self-parenting, we can learn to believe in new possibilities. Our inner child is terrified of trusting in anyone or anything. We need to calm our inner child and assure him/her that we will be safe if we trust again.

Our inner child also feels betrayed by God. Of course our inner child's view of God is very primitive. As an adult we see God as a force for good at work in the universe. Some of us see God as the force of love energy in the universe. Most of us do not see God as a punishing being, but our inner child sees God that way. We need to help our inner child understand that God is a force for good. We need to use self-soothing exercises to help our inner child move toward faith again.

Step Two allows for the possibility of recovery. To transform our lives, we need to believe that we can change them for the better in spite of a history of codependency or trauma. We need to believe that change is possible, or we are lost forever. We need to see a possibility for ourselves that is radically different from the one we find ourselves in now, or we are doomed to repeat the patterns of the past. The second step offers us a chance to believe and create a new life!

Let the Healing Begin

Self-Parenting Affirmations

God is with me always,
I am protected.

I let go and let God,
knowing all my needs will be met.

God takes care of everyone,
including everyone I love.

Self-Soothing Exercises that
Repair and Restore: A Centering Word

Choose a two-syllable word. It might be a word that makes you feel good, like *sunshine*; or something that you like to drink, like *cocoa*; or something that makes you feel peaceful; or something that you enjoy doing (like fishing); or your name; or the name of someone important to you. Or it could just be a made-up word that feels good to say. The important thing is that it is two syllables and that it is a positive word for you.

The key to using a centering word is to tie your word to your breath.

- Begin with a deep breath.

- Say to yourself (not out loud), one syllable as you inhale and one syllable as you exhale. Say this simply, gently, without stress or tension. One syllable as you inhale, one syllable as you exhale.

- Look into the near distance, about five feet, your eyes softly focused; or close your eyes. Do this for a minute. Breathe in and out and say your syllables, gently moving other thoughts out of your mind as you think only of your word.

- Note the effects of this brief practice. Notice the reduction of tension in your body as you do this practice. Notice how good you feel with only this limited time devoted to taking care of yourself.

- Plan for how you can take the minute or two utilized by this practice several times a day—at your desk, in the restroom, as you are waking up in the morning, as you put yourself to sleep. See how you can find small amounts of time to relax yourself.

- Try to find time to lengthen this practice for up to twenty minutes a day. Begin where you are and derive the benefits from what you are currently doing.

 ## Codependency Connection

Compulsive self-reliance is an outgrowth of codependency. When we are traumatized, our need to be self-reliant is increased and becomes a safety issue. We need to recognize that compulsive self-reliance is a coping mechanism and we can stop it, but we need to self-parent and use our intellect to remind our inner child that we are not alone. It would be helpful if you keep track of times when you are being compulsively self-reliant—times when you feel you have to take care of everything by yourself with no help from others. Stop yourself, and write down your feelings. Ask yourself what your inner child needs. This how you will learn to self-parent.

 ## My Journal

Write down how you exhibit compulsive self-reliance in your life. Where do you see areas where you can make changes?

Write down your current ideas about God:

- Do you have a positive relationship with God?
- Do you feel betrayed by God?
- What kind of relationship would you like to have?

Sometimes we need to speak to God but don't quite know how to begin, and that's where a prayer can help. For a "Letting Go" prayer, visit www.ogormandiaz.com.

CHAPTER 9

&

STEP THREE:

We Let Go of Toxic Loyalty and Let Our Higher Power Guide Us

We are not human beings having a spiritual experience. We are spiritual beings having a human experience.

—PIERRE TEILHARD DE CHARDIN, FRENCH JESUIT AND PHILOSOPHER

*B*arbara felt as though everyone was using her: her family, her friends, even her boyfriend. And she just took it. She stayed with her boyfriend even after she caught him cheating on her with one of her so-called friends. She visited her mom a couple of times a week, even though every time she visited, her mom would berate her for not achieving more, not being married or having a better job, or *not dressing better. It didn't matter what it was, her mother found something to put her down for. And even though Barbara got angry at her mother, she also felt bad for her. Her mother had been crippled in a horrible car accident that had also killed her dad. Barbara had witnessed the accident, which happened in front of her middle school when she was ten.*

Her parents had picked her up from her field hockey practice and they had planned to go out for an early dinner at the pizza house when they were blindsided by a drunk driver. Barbara always blamed herself for the accident. She felt that horrible day wouldn't have happened if her parents hadn't needed to come to her school to pick her up. What she didn't know was that on the day of the accident, her mother, who was driving, had also been drinking.

Her mother drank excessively now, which she blamed on the pain from the accident. When she got very drunk, she would remind Barbara that if they hadn't needed to pick her up, her father would still be alive. Since Barbara felt responsible for the accident, she felt she was bound to care for her mother for the rest of her life.

No matter where Barbara looked, she felt trapped. She had no clue about how to change her life.

Dr. Lillian Glass, author of *Toxic People* (1995), describes a toxic person as "anyone who manages to drag you down, makes you feel angry, worn out, deflated, belittled, or confused. . . . It may be difficult for people to admit they are in a toxic relationship, because they are intelligent, self-sufficient individuals in other aspects of their lives. Most people in toxic relationships, however, have the sense that something is just not right."

Step Three is an action step. It is the step where we turn over our will and our lives to a higher power and let go of our toxic loyalty. (For a list of ways to tell if your relationship is toxic, visit www .ogormandiaz.com.) This is a major action for a trauma survivor or codependent to take, because our inner child rebels at the thought of trusting in anyone or anything other than ourselves. This step means letting go and letting God. It means letting go of our complete self-reliance, and instead letting a power greater than ourselves move in our lives.

Even after receiving treatment for our trauma, even after the pain and memories recede, we still have old habits of behavior that we need to break. Our inner child has relied on our perseverance and intelligence to maintain an illusion of safety. Our inner child has controlled us in an effort to avoid being traumatized again; he or she has tried to keep us safe from harm.

However, we cannot live in fear if we expect to live a happy life. We must stop our inner child from constantly controlling our lives with fear. When we are conditioned to fear, it is difficult to imagine a world where we can feel safe and secure. Our belief system is based on what we have previously experienced. Changing our belief system with no evidence that we will be taken care of takes a huge leap of faith. We need to free ourselves from our compulsive self-reliance to be able to take Step Three.

Dependence Is a Dirty Word

We need to create a bridge from a traumatic past to a fulfilling present. We need to let a higher power—or in our case, a higher parent—take over our lives. We must learn to depend on someone greater than ourselves. That is a tall order for someone who has had his or her trust violated! For a trauma survivor, letting go of self-will feels like being utterly unprotected. Only by letting go of our absolute reliance on self-will and reaching out to God or our higher parent can we take the first steps to freeing the child within.

For those with codependence, it is especially difficult to let go and rely on a higher power or parent. Dependence is a dirty word for anyone who has been traumatized or is a codependent. When we think of depending on anyone else, fear of betrayal rears its ugly head.

Toxic Family Loyalty

There is probably no stronger bond than the one that we have to our family of origin. This is especially true for trauma survivors. In an alcoholic family or one where there has been sexual abuse, the rule is to maintain secrecy. This secrecy is all based on shame, and it is a form of blackmail: if you tell the family secret, you will be excluded or expelled from the family. In our practices we've heard too many stories of someone who was abused in his or her family and decided to expose the abuse and was then punished by the family for protecting him- or herself and exposing the family secret. This is also true for children of alcoholics who talk about parental addiction; they are punished for telling the truth.

It is hard for us to judge our family's behavior with any objectivity. Only after we grow older and see other families at work are we able to have a judgment standard. It is also important to remember that as children, we were completely dependent on our family, and challenging their behavior can have far-reaching consequences.

One of the biggest fears of childhood is being abandoned by our family. We believe that even a bad family is better than no family at all.

Fear of Being Abandoned

Codependency is based in fear. Codependency is all about being safe. That is why we stay in toxic relationships; even when our relationships don't work for us, in our codependent thinking, a bad partner is better than no partner. Our greatest fear is being abandoned. Until we believe that we alone are enough, until we feel safe just with ourselves, we will be slaves to the fear of being abandoned. Fear is the enemy! Fear is debilitating; it leaves you hopeless and chronically anxious. Fear sucks the joy out of you and leaves you unable to relax and feel protected. Fear can literally kill you.

The fact is fear is self-imposed. Fear is a choice. We can live without fear if we learn to control how we think. Fear is not outside us, it is but a reaction to experience. Fear is born from our negative experiences and negative expectations. Whether the cause is physical or mental abuse or being a witness to a horrible event, fear is an aftermath of our experience.

When we live in fear, we create a world filled with threats and potential harm. We live in the world we believe exists. But the choice is ours: we can live in a world of terror and lack, or we can live in a world where we have support, safety, and abundance. We create our world and we have the ability to choose how that world is going to be from this day forward. Ask yourself, "What am I choosing?"

Most of us learn to accept fear as a logical response to a scary situation. Most of us are taught that we should prepare for the worst in life. Unfortunately, when we prepare for the worst, the worst is what we attract. What we think about is what we create. If we expect positive outcomes, we receive positive situations . . . but if we have a habit of negative thinking, we create negativity in our lives. We create our reality with our thoughts and our expectations.

One of the most difficult things for trauma survivors and those with codependence to do is to live in the present and not in the past. When you have only experienced negative outcomes in the past, it is extremely difficult to let go and expect positive outcomes in your future. Living in the *now* is difficult for trauma survivors, but living in the *now* is what is necessary to heal and move on.

There are two acronyms for the word "fear": **F**alse **E**vidence **A**ppearing **R**eal and **F**orgetting **E**verything's **A**ll **R**ight. Keep those sayings in mind whenever you feel fear rising up within you.

Our Higher Power

Fear creates fear scenarios, but faith creates faith scenarios. Many of us are angry with God; we feel betrayed and abandoned by any spiritual protection. It has not been our experience that a power greater than ourselves exists. It was not there as far as we could see when we were abused and traumatized. Yet upon reflection, we may see the hand of a higher power in our lives. After all, we survived our trauma, whether it was a war, a rape, violence in our childhood, or a natural disaster. There was a comfort that we were able to hold on to during the worst of times.

Our will has not been able to stop us from our unhealthy compulsions. We drank, took drugs, ended up in repetitive destructive relationships, and either ate compulsively or had eating disorders we did not control. But if we let go and let God, and we give over the control of our life to our higher power, we create faith scenarios full of safety, love, and joy. As we discussed earlier, the higher power is the intuitive knowledge within each of us. It is the part connected to our spiritual source, or, as some say, the universal consciousness or God. If we adopt the concept of a higher power connected to a greater consciousness, it is easier to let go. If we rely on a source greater than ourselves, we can learn to self-nurture while never really being alone again. If we can see our higher power as the spiritual core of what we are, we can ease the anxiety of letting go of reliance on self, and let a greater aspect of what we are take more control in our lives.

If we can think of our higher power this way, we can see that the inner child is not replaced but is now being nurtured by another aspect of self that is not connected to the ego or to the pain of the past. The higher power seeks only solutions, and it guides behavior that leads to growth. We come to understand that the universe is inevitably moving toward fulfillment with the higher parent as the guide.

Unfortunately, the concept of authority for many of us is laden with all kinds of negative connotations. We need to understand that God as a higher authority is in no way similar to our birth parents. God has no other agenda than our well-being! The Universe is an ocean of love flowing in the direction of joy and healing. God and our higher parent is a cornucopia of abundance made to supply our every need. That higher self—the divine within us—moves us into new paths fueled by faith and guided by a greater intelligence. Using our courage, we bend toward God and take risks we never took before, from seeking professional help to joining a self-help group.

When we let our higher power in, we enter new territory. We are no longer totally invested in protecting ourselves. We can experience the world as a safe place. We learn to live in the present moment.

Self-Parenting for Healing

It is important to nurture your inner child through the process of letting go of toxic loyalty. Your inner child will react to letting go of people in your life that he or she has become accustomed to. Change is always hard for the inner child, and your input as the adult with reason is needed to guide you through the process. Your inner child will also need to be calmed down as you move a higher power back into your life. Remember that she has a child's view of God. And in her mind, God betrayed her.

~

Let the Healing Begin

~

Self-Parenting Affirmations

*I am whole and complete
as I am.*

*I am a God-filled being,
and I trust others because they, too,
are God-filled beings.*

*I can never be abandoned because
God is with me always.*

~

Self-Soothing Exercises that Repair and Restore: Let Go and Let God

To let go of toxic loyalty, you will need help. That help means being willing to trust in a higher power. In your journal:

Write a letter describing your fears about letting go and letting God.

- Describe your response to the notion that "fear" is **F**alse **E**vidence **A**ppearing **R**eal, or **F**orgetting **E**verything's **A**ll **R**ight

 ## The Codependency Connection

Codependency is all about inappropriate loyalty. Loyalty has been the hallmark of our lives, leaving us exhausted and betrayed. Trauma survivors and those with codependence also have a hard time relying on anyone or anything, especially God. We will have to challenge our old patterns to move from toxic loyalty to independence and from self-reliance to reliance on God. As you begin this process, write down your experiences with learning to rely on a higher power.

 ## My Journal

As you chart your recovery, it is important to examine all of your relationships. You must ensure that all relationships are reciprocal. If you are to build a new life, you need to weed

out those relationships to which you have been loyal in spite
of evidence that they are harmful to you. You need to go
through the real but misguided feeling that you are betraying
others, because in reality you are only being true to yourself. Ask yourself the following questions and describe your
thoughts and feelings about each one in your journal:

- Do you find yourself questioning why you are involved
  with your partner?

- Do you have a bottom line that you hold to regarding
  relationships?

- Is it hard for you to determine when to stand up
  for yourself?

- Is it hard for you to determine when to leave a
  relationship?

- Do you feel that you must support your family even
  when you know they are wrong?

- Is it hard for you to "let go and let God"?

- Can you imagine feeling the security of never being
  alone as long as you have God in your life?

Asking God for help is often difficult when we've experienced trauma and are codependent. Prayer is a personal and
intimate way to speak with God that many people find helpful.
Visit www.ogormandiaz.com for a "Prayer for Protection."

༄

CHAPTER 10

STEP FOUR:

We Made an Inventory of Our Assets and Deficits Regarding Our Trauma and Codependency

Forgiveness is a way of life that gradually transforms us from being helpless victims of our circumstances to being powerful and loving co-creators of our reality.

—ROBIN CASARJIAN FROM *FORGIVENESS: A BOLD CHOICE FOR A PEACEFUL HEART*

*N*ancy finally felt she might make headway in her healing. "I was so confused. I knew as a child that I was affected by watching my mother fall apart as her mental illness got worse. Her parenting* *got more bizarre, from locking me in my room for hours to multiple suicide attempts. But I thought that was behind me when I became an adult. Then I married John, and after he returned from Iraq, he was a mess. He'd wake up screaming at night, which scared the kids and me. And when he got treatment and started getting better, I got hit by a car. I was in chronic pain for months.*

"I didn't know where to start. Finally, I found a therapist who understood complex trauma and was able to help me sort things out. I came to understand that I had developed many strengths as well as deficits from my experiences. Growing up in a home like mine also helped me become resilient, which has helped me become successful as a parent, a wife, and at work. In a strange way, I am grateful for all the negative things that have happened to me, because they made me who I am today—and I like who I am today!"

Like Nancy, if we are to move beyond our codependency and trauma, we need to figure out our history and become clear on what happened to us and what effect it had on us. Once we have accomplished that, we can repair the broken places and build on the strong places.

Post-Traumatic Stress Inventory

Post-traumatic stress can be a major factor for trauma survivors. It is important to identify your post-traumatic stress symptoms and develop a way to deal with them. If you were the victim of a traumatic episode, write in your journal about what happened, the age you were when it happened, and how you felt.

Post-Traumatic Stress Trauma
Symptoms and Triggers

In Chapter 1, we discussed symptoms that are common for those experiencing post-traumatic stress. After reviewing that list on pages 23–26, write in your journal about the symptoms you identify with, and add others that are not on the list.

In your journal, list those triggers that spark your post-traumatic stress symptoms.

Learned Helplessness

We learn to become helpless through the messages we were given as children from our families. Learned helplessness is a way of thinking that often leads to depression. Victims of learned helplessness believe they cannot control what happens to them; they learn to be pessimistic. Children who are taught to be optimistic learn that bad things are only temporary and as individuals they can impact their environment. One model teaches empowering beliefs, the other teaches disempowering beliefs.

Learned Helplessness Inventory

In your journal, list your answers to each of the following questions:

1. What disempowering beliefs were you taught as a child?
2. What disempowering beliefs do you still have?
3. What empowering beliefs can you replace them with? If you aren't sure what to write, begin with turning your negative beliefs listed above into positive statements.

Complex Trauma

As we discussed in Part One, complex trauma is repeated abuse over time. Whether the abuse happened in childhood, adulthood, or both, the identifying factor for complex trauma is that it is repeated trauma. One significant symptom is that many victims of complex trauma continue to put themselves in high-risk situations, which often lead to revictimization. It is important to identify complex trauma when it happens so the cycle of trauma and victimization can be interrupted.

Complex Trauma Inventory

In your journal, write down your answers to the following:

1. Make a list of the times that you can remember being traumatized. Be specific and complete.
2. How did complex trauma negatively affect you?
3. What strengths did you derive from being exposed to trauma?

Secondary Trauma

As we discussed previously, secondary trauma is also known as compassion fatigue. Whether we are counselors, firefighters, child welfare workers, nurses, or doctors, almost anyone can potentially experience secondary trauma. It is important to identify secondary trauma because it is subtle. Remember that secondary trauma can be as destructive as acute trauma and must be recognized and treated.

Secondary Trauma Inventory

Write your answers to the following questions in your journal:

1. Have you witnessed traumatic events that happened to others? What were the incidents? How did they negatively affect you?
2. How did those same incidents positively affect you?
3. Have you been told about traumatic events by others either professionally or by a friend? Write about how you felt when you first heard about them.
4. How did hearing about those traumatic events affect you later?
5. Do you ever feel that you are emotionally exhausted from all the sadness around you? Describe your feelings.

Intergenerational or Historical Trauma

Historical trauma is obvious to some people but not apparent to others. If you are Jewish, African American, Native American, or Japanese American, the cultural oppression faced by your people is obvious.

Intergenerational or Historical Trauma Inventory

Explore the impact of intergenerational or historical trauma on you and your family by journaling the answers to the following:

1. Have you or your ancestors been victimized or oppressed because of your race, cultural group, socioeconomic status, or gender? In what ways?
2. How do you feel about those victimizations?

3. Have you experienced self-hate because of cultural or religious oppression, socioeconomic status, parenting practices, gender?

4. Have your parents' experiences of racism, religious oppression, poverty, cultural oppression, or poor parenting impacted you? If so, how?

5. Do you feel disconnected from your cultural roots? If so, why?

6. In what way that increases your self-esteem are you proud of your religion, social group, family, cultural group, or race?

7. What strengths did you derive as a victim of intergenerational trauma?

Resilience

As we've learned, we also develop strengths from adversity. We develop resilience by creating internal scaffolding, an inner structure with steps and resting places that allows us to put our trauma and codependency in a place within us where they can be both understood and contained.

Resilience Inventory

Some of the strengths we develop through adversity are humor, intelligence, the ability to plan, and perseverance. In your journal, list all your strengths, noting especially those born from your childhood experiences.

Self-Parenting for Healing

We need to know what we need to change, and we do that by making an inventory. Making an inventory allows us to take stock. It allows us to get realistic concerning our strengths and weakness.

We will usually find out that we have more going for us than against us. Then we can see what strengths we can use to remedy our weaknesses. The inventory is one of the most important things you can do for your recovery!

∾

Let the Healing Begin

∾

Self-Parenting Affirmations

I can focus on containing my triggers,
putting them aside every time
they begin to call me.

The past is past and I live in the now.

I am the change I want to be.

Life begins right now as I re-create myself.

I am free of the past and I create my future.

∾

Self-Soothing Exercises that Repair and Restore: Learn to Control Your Body and Mind

Just as you have reviewed where you are holding yourself back and where you are finding strength, you can review the same with your body.

- Lie on your back in a comfortable position. Allow your arms to rest at your sides, palms down, on the surface next to you.

- Inhale and exhale slowly and deeply.

- Clench your hands into fists and hold them tightly for fifteen seconds. As you do this, relax the rest of your body. Visualize your fists contracting, becoming tighter and tighter.

- Then let your hands relax, making all your muscles in your hand soft and flexible.

- Now, tense and relax the following parts of your body in this order: face, shoulders, back, stomach, pelvis, legs, feet, and toes. Hold each part tensed for fifteen seconds and then relax your body for thirty seconds before going on to the next part.

- Finish the exercise by shaking your hands and imagining the remaining tension flowing out of your fingertips.

Do this as part of daily self-care. In a pinch, do one part of your body as you feel yourself beginning to tense. No one will even know you are doing this!

The Codependency Connection

Remember, codependency is learned behavior. What is learned can be unlearned. Search out your codependent behaviors, then write them down and add them to your chart as we discussed in Step One. Once we identify toxic behaviors, we ensure that we do not have to carry forward what we were taught in the past.

My Journal

We must have a clear vision for achieving our goal of health and abundance. First we identify the pain and its effects. Then we define our assets and deficits, our strengths and weakness. Then we develop a plan to remedy our problems and learn how to live our lives instead of our stories. In your journal, create lists for each of the following:

- Deficits
- Strengths
- Resources needed but not currently available
- Changes needed
- Relationships that need to change
- New relationships that need to be developed

CHAPTER 11

꩜

STEP FIVE:

We Learned to Forgive Ourselves and Others as a Way to Move On

Your own self-realization is the greatest service you can render the world.

—RAMANA MAHARSHI

*J*uan was tired of hating and feeling angry. He was thirty-five years old, and hate and anger had consumed him for too long. He was raped by his uncle when he was seven, and saw his father killed by a drunk driver when he was twelve. Because his father was black and his mother was Latina, he was constantly facing racism. His world felt like one big war. His wife had left him, and her final words were an accusation that he would never be able to have a healthy relationship because his heart was so closed. And he knew she was right; his *heart was closed. Juan realized that unless he could learn to forgive his uncle, the person who killed his father, and himself, he would live a loveless life.*

He sought the help of a therapist, and learned that forgiveness isn't letting people off the hook; forgiveness means holding people responsible without attachment. "I never realized how much energy it takes to hate," Juan confessed. "There is no room for anything else. I really did not realize that I have a choice. I thought the way I reacted to the situations in my life was normal. I learned that it's healthy for me to leave my trauma behind and my anger with it. I found out that I was living my trauma every day of my life through my anger, and it was making me miserable."

Step Five challenges us to learn to forgive ourselves and others. Forgiveness is about having a sense of peaceful resolution when there has been good reason to have negative emotions.

Forgiveness allows us to finally leave the past in the past and not feel the pain of trauma again and again. Many of us feel that each time we have a memory, we are retraumatized. Some people feel as though they have been traumatized hundreds of times, because with each memory or flashback, they experience everything anew.

Forgiveness is often described as a state of letting go, a process of releasing the past and moving forward into the future. It is the recognition that until we let go, the abuse still has power over us. Forgiveness is really not about what it does for the other person, but what it does for the survivor. But we must be careful not to forgive our tormentors too early. We must take care of ourselves first.

Blame

Blame does have some positive aspects. When we blame, we give meaning to what happened to us. We try to make sense of terrible things, and sometimes the only way to find meaning is to blame ourselves. This is what happens for many trauma victims or those with codependency. If we can blame ourselves for what happened, we can ascribe some meaning to a cruel and meaningless event. Blame gives order to a seemly chaotic universe.

A woman might say, "He wouldn't have raped me if I hadn't been wearing a short dress or walked home through that dark alley." A young child might say, "If I wasn't bad at school, my dad wouldn't drink." This process is called internalized blame. We feel that if we are in some way responsible, then there was a reason for the abuse or other traumatic situation. Often we blame ourselves if someone dies in war and we were unable to save him or her; or a rape occurs and we feel we contributed to the circumstances that led to it; or an accident happens and we feel in some way we should have been able to stop it from happening. And of course, all of this is unrealistic. But self-blame, as we said before, does allow us to make sense of the trauma.

Anger

At least in the beginning, anger was helpful to us. It gave us the energy to keep functioning after we were traumatized. Anger also gave us focus, a place to put our pain. The fantasy of revenge made us feel less helpless.

Many of us who have been traumatized think our anger will somehow take away our pain. But by keeping our trauma so present with our anger, we are forced to relive our trauma every day. The fact is, trauma doesn't exist in the present—it exists in the past! The problem is by staying in a state of anger, we keep the trauma ever present. We need our anger for a while, but at some point we need to put it aside and learn forgiveness if we are going to leave the past behind.

Why We Shouldn't Forgive Right Away

True forgiveness does not come easily. In some cases, forgiving too early is destructive. It is important to process our trauma before we forgive, because forgiveness is not an intellectual process: it is an emotional and spiritual process. When we are trying to deal with just feeling safe again, and we are busy managing our terror, it is important just to feel we have some control over our lives. Before we forgive, we need to build a safe world and be able to manage the flashbacks and triggers that overwhelm us.

We need to allow ourselves healing time. We need to self-soothe and learn first to forgive ourselves before we can forgive anyone else. We need to forgive any misconception that we are in any way responsible for what happened to us. When we realize that we did the best we could with what we had, and we are in no way responsible for the trauma we experienced, we take a major step toward freedom from trauma, and that is when we may be ready to forgive others.

Forgiving Others Who Hurt Us

Most people don't understand the complex situations and feelings that trauma survivors and codependents experience. Sometimes other people may seem callous or say insensitive things to us and unintentionally cause pain for us. Even family members may become inpatient with us and cause us pain when our trauma seems to linger too long.

Sometimes we subject others to some of our trauma reactions. These are often good people who don't understand our triggers or why we respond in a negative way to what they thought was a harmless comment or action. Sometimes these people are friends or coworkers, sometimes they are family members. But they can be anyone, even strangers. In either case, as we heal, we need to create a list of people to forgive for hurting us unintentionally.

Forgiving the Perpetrator

The most difficult aspect of trauma is when—if ever—to forgive the perpetrator. It is not necessary to forgive the perpetrator in order to begin your recovery. But over the long term, the only way to release yourself from any control the perpetrator may have over you is to practice forgiveness.

Remember that forgiveness is different from not holding people responsible; we need to hold our perpetrators responsible. We need to testify if we have to, to help incarcerate those who hurt us or others. But we can do this in the spirit of forgiveness. We can hold people responsible in a spirit of detachment.

When we are ready, we let go of our anger and forgive, knowing that those who hurt us are sick people. As we forgive, the sting of the past is released, and we truly become free!

Self-Parenting for Healing

Forgiveness is always a hard process for trauma survivors and codependents. Our inner child rebels at the idea that we forgive. It is very hard to give up righteous anger. It is important to remember that forgiveness is not for others—it's for us. We need to help our inner child understand that forgiveness is part of our healing. Forgiveness allows us to truly put the pain from the past to rest. Once we release our rage and resentment, we open our hearts to love.

Let the Healing Begin

Self-Parenting Affirmations

I forgive myself for being a child and for being so very vulnerable to all who took care of me.

I can again enjoy the freedom I felt as a child; this is a safe journey for me.

I can protect myself now and use this protection when painful memories of the past arise.

I can be the parent I never had while I also mourn this loss.

Self-Soothing Exercises that Repair and Restore: Learn to Create Inner Safety

Being safe is a core need for trauma survivors and code-pendents. This exercise allows you to create a safe place whenever you need one. It's a portable safety net!

- See yourself in your safe place. Picture a tranquil scene. For example, see yourself in a tree if you are picturing a mountain or a valley scene, or nestled in a sand dune if you are picturing the ocean, or under a palm tree if you are seeing an island. What is important is that you can visualize yourself there.
- Next, bring to yourself elements that will make you feel even safer. Visualize a protector or two, or ten; these might be a bear, for example, or an eagle, or a hawk, a kindly teacher, a guidance counselor from your youth, even angels. Bring in as many elements as you wish. The goal is to make this a safe place for you.
- See yourself in your safe place, surrounded by those elements that will make you safe.
- See yourself doing something that is relaxing: reading, watching the water, whatever is relaxing for you to do.

Visualize yourself in your safe place as many times a day as you need to. Relish your ability to take care of yourself in this way. Think of this particularly when you are feeling stress, have just been triggered, or need to rest.

Codependency Connection

Perhaps the hardest thing for trauma survivors who are codependents to do is to forgive. We have been unjustly treated. We have been abused, yet we are obligated, for our own recovery, to forgive the very people who have injured us.

We must also forgive ourselves for our controlling behavior. As an adaptation of growing up in a dysfunctional home, we became control freaks. We became control freaks to get some order, some predictability in our lives. We may have hurt others, but most of the time we were simply trying to survive, and we intended no one harm. We need to give ourselves a break; we need to forgive ourselves. Write down your thoughts about your need for control. Try to identify when you feel out of control. Ask yourself what triggers your need for control.

 My Journal

As part of your recovery plan, you need to make a forgiveness list. In your journal, write the name of each person who you need to forgive and why you need to forgive them. Write a forgiveness statement for each person. As part of your healing process, say each forgiveness out loud.

Asking God or your higher power to help you forgive yourself or another person will help you feel connected to the universe and aid in your recovery. For a "Forgiveness" prayer, visit www.ogormandiaz.com.

❧

CHAPTER 12

STEP SIX:

We Claimed Our Strength and Embraced Our Resilience

In the deserts of the heart
Let the healing fountain start,
In the prison of his days
Teach the free man how to praise.

—W. H. AUDEN, FROM
"IN MEMORY OF W. B. YEATS"

*M*ark was proud of his new promotion. After a lifetime of adversity, he finally felt like a success, like things were finally going his way. In fact, when he thought about it, he kind of owed his success to his crappy childhood. After all, if he hadn't been exposed to so much adversity, he wouldn't be who he was today.

If it hadn't been for his mother's mental illness, he would not have learned how to take care of himself at a young age and develop the self-confidence and independence he now possessed. In a very real way, he was grateful to her, even though at the time he resented having to be on his own so much. Actually, when he thought about it, most of his positive attributes were in some way tied to the struggles he faced early in life. In fact, if he had not been traumatized, he would not have the sense of inner strength he now did.

Mark knew it hadn't been all his accomplishment; his close relationship to his high-school coach allowed him to find a surrogate parent. The fact that sports were so important to him in high school gave him a different peer group than the gangbangers in his neighborhood. A life that started out to be a tragedy ended up with a happy ending!

Resilience is described variously as the ability to bounce back from adversity or as effective coping under stress. It has also been said that resiliency is the ability to maintain optimism, hope, and self-motivation in the face of adversity. Many of us have developed resilient coping strategies to meet the challenges that we face as a result of being traumatized as children. Many people who experienced trauma become stronger and more successful than the average person who has not faced adversity.

Some of us had protective factors such as high intelligence or supportive adults, which helped support resilience. Resilient people are those who are generally optimistic, have a good sense of humor and self-worth, are goal-oriented, adaptable, and have a supportive social network. Spirituality, such as belief and reliance on a higher power, reduces trauma and supports resilience, as do traits such as seeing oneself as a survivor rather than a victim, and having good problem-solving skills.

Nothing is completely black or white. Even the most horrific situations can have some positive outcomes. Those of us who have thrived in spite of painful experiences need to celebrate our positive outcomes. In a way, honoring our heroism and optimism in the face of adversity is in itself a victory over our trauma and those who violated us. We who have not only survived but thrived in spite of it all are winners!

Resiliency Styles

In Chapter 4, Dr. Patricia O'Gorman shared a new paradigm for defining resilience. In your journal, explore and write about these resiliency styles as part of your healing process. Which type of resilience do you identify with? ·

Paradoxical. Having skills that are only used in one part of one's life—for instance, being effective managers at work but not at home. *Personal Growth Goal:* Use skills in all areas of life. Describe how you intend to do this.

Stellar. Knowing you have survived a trauma and being proud of that, but being unable to move into an expanded sense of self. *Personal Growth Goal:* Expand how you view yourself. Describe what an expanded view might look like.

Self-Contained. Identifying as resilient and being proud of that but not developing other parts of your identity. *Personal Growth Goal:* Focus on showing your vulnerable side. Describe your fears and hopes, and how you can share with people you trust.

Underdeveloped. You have not developed your strengths because you have not been allowed to. *Personal Growth Goal:* Develop a number of resilience skills to improve your coping skills and self-worth. Write down a list of strengths you would like to develop and describe how you can accomplish this.

Overwhelmed. A recent trauma has made it difficult or impossible to access your resilience. *Personal Growth Goal:* Learn that this is temporary and you will be okay soon. List your resilience skills and know that you will access them again soon.

Balanced. Your resiliency skills are available to you and you use them in your daily life. Journal about how your life looks when you are balanced.

Self-Parenting for Healing

Your inner child will resonate with the recognition that you have gained many positive adaptations to your traumatic past. This is a time to celebrate and consolidate your strengths. It is important to acknowledge that you have not only survived a dysfunctional, traumatic childhood, but you have thrived and excelled. As you self-parent, remember to see all the positive parts of your personality that have helped you through your trauma and codependency.

~

Let the Healing Begin

Self-Parenting Affirmations

Adversity has made me stronger.

I have strengths and I use them to be successful.

I am a loyal and loving person.

I am already a success.

I am getting better and better every day.

Self-Soothing Exercises that Repair and Restore: Slowing Time

One of the principles of healing is that slowing time is a good idea. It is a particularly good technique to use when you become aware that you are feeling anxious. When we become anxious, we have a tendency to "speed up." You can counter this by consciously slowing yourself down.

- **Breathe slower.** Consciously slowing your breathing when you feel your heart is racing can be a very effective way to feel conscious control.

- **Drive five miles under the speed limit.** You can consciously take control of how fast you allow yourself to drive and even rejoice in it (though this might feel like torture for some of you!). But try it, because you may find that when others are passing you by in their desperate efforts to get somewhere two minutes sooner, you might actually be freed to take a deep breath.

- **Talk slower.** When you are feeling pressured, there is a natural tendency to want to speak faster and cram more in. Doing just the opposite can give you a measure of control. And it will allow you to collect your thoughts so that you are saying what you mean to say—not less, not more.

- **Move more slowly.** There is an old adage that has a great deal of truth in it: *The faster you go, the longer it will take to get there*. When you hurry, you are more likely to make mistakes, break something, take a wrong turn, or forget something. So move slowly, and if you are already tense, move very slowly and consciously. Consciously take control of your time. Take the extra minute to be prepared, to be safe, and to ensure you are moving in the right direction.

- **Slow your thinking.** When you feel your mind is racing, consciously control your thinking. Use your breath to slow your heart rate and focus your thoughts. Select what you want to think about, and block what you do not want to think about. Use the techniques we have discussed thus far to assist you.

 ## Codependency Connection

Codependency, like trauma, has positive as well as negative outcomes. While we want to move away from the negative aspects of our current codependency, we can still find something useful among the original negative experiences and our adaptations to them. We are loyal, hardworking, and creative. We are responsible people who have compassion. We are strong people made stronger by adversity. Take stock of what codependency has done for you. Make a list of positive aspects of your codependent behavior that have served you well.

 My Journal

In your journal, add your resiliency traits to any previous lists and describe how you intend to utilize those traits in the future. Consolidate the positive aspects of your codependency while continuing to work on letting go of the negative aspects. Remember that good things came from your traumatic past and you need to celebrate them!

CHAPTER 13

❧

STEP SEVEN:

We Became Ready to Overcome Intergenerational Trauma and Codependency Through Self-Awareness and Self-Parenting

*There are only two mistakes one can
make along the road to truth:
Not going all the way, and not starting.*

—BUDDHA

*I*t is our way to mourn for one year when one of our relations enters the spirit world. Tradition is to wear black when mourning our loved one. Tradition is to not be happy, not to sing and dance and enjoy life's beauties during mourning time. Tradition is to suffer with

171

the remembering of our lost ones and to give away much of what we own and to cut our hair short. Chief Sitting Bull was more than a relation. He represented an entire people, our freedom, and our way of life, all that we were. For 100 years, we as a people have mourned our great leader. We have followed tradition in our mourning. We have not been happy, have not enjoyed life's beauty, have not danced or sung as a proud nation. We have suffered, remembering our great chief, and have given away much of what was ours. Blackness has been around us for one-hundred years. During this time the heartbeat of our people has been weak and our lifestyle has deteriorated to a devastating degree. Our people now suffer from the highest rates of unemployment, poverty, alcoholism and suicide in this country.

—R. C. BLACKCLOUD (1990)

For many of us, trauma and codependency are multigenerational. They haven't just happened to us—they've happened to our mothers and fathers and grandparents. This is particularly true for Native Americans, Holocaust survivors, and children of alcoholics, all of whom have well-documented intergenerational trauma. As we've noted in earlier chapters, there is another, more subtle form of trauma that we must consider for some codependents who are trauma survivors: historical and intergenerational trauma, which is the cumulative emotional and psychological wounding across generations.

We experience this type of trauma vicariously by being told about it. All of the symptoms of trauma are true for people affected by historical trauma and intergenerational trauma, just as they are for secondary trauma. Suicide, addiction, anxiety, rage, and other self-destructive behaviors are all present with intergenerational trauma. The trauma an individual experiences in an earlier generation can affect the lives of future generations. For example, a pattern of maternal abandonment of a child at a young age might be seen across three generations in the same way as a pattern of alcoholism is.

Children of Jews who experienced the Holocaust are victims of secondary trauma because they have heard stories about the trauma of the concentration camps, and experienced the deep changes that occurred in some who then became parents. There also is evidence that children of trauma victims are hardwired to inherit PTSD. This research continues, but it is clear that the release of cortisol *in utero* can create a biological proclivity for trauma (Yehuda, Halligan, and Grossman 2001).

Transmitting Trauma

Research shows that a parent can vicariously and unintentionally transmit their traumatic experiences of interpersonal violence through their behaviors and narrative associations (Schechter 2005). In other words, using verbal and nonverbal signs, parents can transfer their prior experiences of violence to their children, who may or may not have been present during those violent events.

In our experience, we've observed that parents who have been traumatized have much higher levels of anxiety, so they tend to overprotect their children and cause anxiety disorders in their children. In this way they create an environment that nurtures hypervigilance and fear in the next generation.

We also have found that another psychological response to trauma is distancing. Failure to show emotional attachment to one's children is a symptom of trauma, especially for groups of people who have lost their relatives to suicide or violence, like concentration camp survivors and Native Americans. This leaves the children feeling punished. For trauma survivors, distancing is a protective mechanism. They believe that if they don't feel love, they can't feel loss. But of course, this mechanism creates children who feel unloved and confused.

In the end, as the family members identify with the trauma, they create trauma throughout the family. Symptoms of trauma are spread intergenerationally though behaviors and verbal transmission. To stop the cycle of trauma and allow healing to begin, every family member must reverse his or her behavior regarding traumatic experiences.

The Gift that Keeps on Giving

Velvet couldn't shake the feeling of sadness she got whenever she thought of her mother as a child. She could sense the pain her mother must have felt when Velvet's granddad, an angry drunk, would rage around the house screaming profanities about the white man and the pain white people caused black people. He would talk about how black people had been abused over generations and how it had impacted him and his family. He yelled that the white man had killed his great-grandfather; a group of Klansmen had beaten him to death. Then he'd rage about how his uncle had died of drug addiction because he could not make it in a white world.

Velvet's grandfather would often get violent when he was drunk and hit her mother. Because she was light-skinned, he accused her of being a white man's child, not his. As well as being the recipient of her father's rage, Velvet's mother, who was the eldest child, took care of her brothers and sisters.

Velvet tried to make up for her mother's childhood by being exceptionally attentive and helpful. When it came time for her to leave home and go to college, Velvet refused the scholarship she had won to an Ivy League college and instead went to the local community college so she could continue to live at home and help her mother. She was not married, and didn't see how she could ever leave her mother.

Velvet suffers from a type of intergenerational trauma where she bears the scar without the wound, and she maintains family ties by integrating her mother's painful experiences. Among other symptoms, those of us with intergenerational trauma develop a need to be overachievers to compensate for our parents' losses. Parents sometimes live vicariously through their children, and it is also true that children live vicariously in the horrific past of their parents. Like Velvet, we develop toxic loyalty to our parents' pain and get stuck in the historical trauma.

If our family cannot support us because they are in so much pain, we must get our support from outside the family. We have observed that children of Holocaust survivors who have outside sources of support like kibbutz, or children of alcoholics who attend Alateen meetings, do better than their contemporaries who rely only on their families.

We must learn to share our experiences as children of trauma survivors with others so we can feel understood and accepted as we are. We must learn to live with love and joy, not fear and negativity. When we are optimistic about our future, then we have won. When we see the world as a wondrous safe place, then we have won. When we see ourselves as spiritual beings who are whole and complete and inviolate, then we have won.

How Healing Takes Place

Healing historical trauma is tricky. It is hard to ignore the pain experienced by people you love. If you are the child of someone who has been treated unjustly, at the very least you are filled with anger. You are also filled with survivor guilt. Therefore, if you are going to heal you must release yourself from guilt for things you could not control. You must reclaim those parts of your culture that have been lost due to trauma. When we take back our history, we repair the cultural pain that was caused by genocide or war. We make a clear statement that we have survived as individuals and as a people.

Our spirituality is an important source of resilience and healing. For Native Americans, this has meant once again going back to traditional ways to anchor them in a positive core of being.

Self-Parenting for Healing

We who are codependent and trauma survivors need to remember that we are heroes. We have won, not lost. We can only lose if we give up on ourselves as individuals and as a people. We must identify with our victories, not our failures, and see ourselves as the warriors we are. We can have compassion without losing ourselves in useless guilt for the pain of others. We can confront the pain and see it as strength. We are more whole, not less, because of the pain. Perhaps the most important thing we can do to overcome intergenerational trauma is to focus on our story of survival instead of our story of trauma and defeat. Once we frame ourselves as those who have overcome and not only survived, but thrived, then we have won the battle over our past pain.

Remember, what happened in your own personal history, as well as what happened in the generational line of your parents, grandparents, great-grandparents, and in your community, is all meaningful. How you handle that is what makes the difference between a life of bitterness and loss and a life of joy and success. Overcoming obstacles like racism, genocide, and violence can create a feeling of worthlessness or one of self-worth—it is up to you!

~

Let the Healing Begin

~

Self-Parenting Affirmations

All my ancestors and I are warriors who fought for the people and won, and we are here!

I have all that I need to be all that I want to be.

No one can take from me my self-respect for who I am.

~

Self-Soothing Exercises that Repair and Restore: Let Go of Shame

We all need to be free from shame and trauma, the twin chains of oppression. We use self-parenting as a defense against shame. When we are able to let go of our generational pain, we can make sense of our entire trauma, including generational trauma.

- Visualize your inner child. Ask him to sit on your knees. Look into his face.

- Tell him that you are taking him away from the pain of the past. Tell him that he no longer has to struggle, that he is free. Tell him that he is a good child, and that no matter what has happened in the past, he is the most lovable and wonderful child in the world.

- Recite those words like a mantra.

- Afterward, write down what you have experienced during the visualization.

- Make this a daily mantra, a cleansing mantra that eliminates shame from your consciousness.

The Codependency Connection

Codependency can be transmitted over time. Our ancestors who were traumatized developed patterns of behavior
based in dysfunctional responses to maltreatment. It has
become natural for some families to have generational
trauma. Our ways of being in the world have been taught to
us over many generations, and we need to recognize that as
we begin our healing process. Make notes to yourself about
your intergenerational pain and how you think you can create
a plan for healing.

 ## My Journal

It is important to understand and put on paper all the ways
we have been traumatized as a people over generations. We
need to chart our generational pain and make that part of
our recovery plan. We need to see our history in perspective
and heal ourselves of generational pain. In your journal, write
about these losses from a generational perspective. Tell the
story of your family over the last three generations, marking
the traumas they faced and noting how these affect you.

❧

CHAPTER 14

STEP EIGHT:

We Left Behind Pessimism and Learned to Become Optimistic

*You don't say "Please forgive me" to the
Divine because the Divine needs to hear it;
you say it because you need to hear it.*

—IHALEAKALA HEW LEN, PH.D., COAUTHOR OF *ZERO LIMITS*

*M*arci needed to change her life, but because of the way she'd been raised, she felt unable to do it. Her mother was always saying things like, "Well, your dad's a drunk and that's it—that will never change," or "We are poor, and poor people stay poor like rich people get richer." Everything bad was part of "the way it was," and there was nothing one could do to change things.

It frustrated Marci to feel so powerless, and she didn't agree that she couldn't have more control over her life. It also troubled her that so many of her friendships were related to work. She was an emergency room nurse and was constantly dealing with the traumas that came in the front door. And when she and her coworkers would go out for a drink, the talk was always about work. Marci felt caged in and wanted to break out and live differently, but she didn't know how.

We learn from our families of origin. The world we live in as children is the world our family tells us exists. Dysfunctional families often teach children to be helpless. Being traumatized or violated at a young age or growing up in a dysfunctional family tends to create learned helplessness. If our parents were pessimistic people, we likely learned to be pessimistic children. If our parents were optimistic, then we probably are, too.

Learned helplessness is created by a perceived absence of control over the outcome of a situation. You believe you are at the mercy of life's travails and can do nothing to change that. You see negative situations as permanent. If you were taught to be helpless, you were taught to accept your fate. Of course this is not true, but if you believe you are helpless, you are. We must leave behind our learned helplessness if we are to create new and productive lives for ourselves. We must learn to be our own cheerleaders!

If we have been traumatized, then our chance to be a victim of learned helplessness increases. Whether it was a rape, a war, an accident, or some other trauma we experienced, it is clear that we were helpless when the incident happened. The impact of being traumatized and being helpless increases the belief that we have no control over what happens to us.

We cannot change our lives unless we feel empowered to do so. We cannot believe in positive change if we don't believe it's possible to change. Allowing learned helplessness to guide our thinking will cripple our chances for success in life. You may have all the talent in the world but if you do not believe in your own ability, you will achieve very little. It is critical to your recovery to learn to be optimistic and to see the world as something you can impact. What was learned in childhood can be unlearned—you don't have to continue to believe untruths.

Positive Psychology

In *Learned Helplessness* (Peterson et al. 1993), the authors teach that much of the depression we experience is due to learned helplessness and the way we have been taught to see the world. Positive psychology asserts that we must learn to control our negative belief system and change the way we view the events and situations in our lives.

Hopefulness, mindfulness, and resilience are all traits of a successful, optimistic person. We must learn to focus our thinking on the positive to combat the negative things we have been taught. Our belief systems determine how we operate in the world—therefore, it is extremely important to control our belief system.

If we have been abused or have witnessed violence, our worldview is colored by those incidents. This trauma-driven belief system is based on fear. When we are traumatized, we have no control over the circumstances. We need to develop a belief system that counters the one that has grown from the trauma.

What disempowering beliefs were you taught as a child? Negative statements like the ones Marci heard growing up are presented as facts, but they create a world where there is no personal power, no way that you as an individual can impact your environment.

Trauma Bonds

As we discussed in Chapter 2, trauma bonds are intense attachments produced as a result of trauma, and they are another aspect of conditioning that we need to counter if we are to get well. They are seen between victim and perpetrator and also between people who have experienced trauma together, like solders or firefighters. Sometimes we bond with these people, sometimes we develop codependency and feel responsible for these people. In either case, we need to review these relationships to ensure that they are healthy.

Check and see how many of your attachments are based on common bad experiences. Ask yourself how much time you spend sharing negative experiences with these people. If your trauma bond is with a perpetrator then it is very important to examine that relationship. It is important that any relationship with the person who abused you does not undermine you in any way.

Self-Parenting for Healing

You have been taught learned helplessness and negativity. Those are learned behaviors. And if you were not born naturally optimistic (as some resilient people are), you will have to work at seeing the world from an optimistic point of view. There is no doubt that optimistic people are more successful. They also live longer and have more fulfilling personal relationships. So why not try optimism?

Your inner child will resist looking at things from a positive point of view. Negativity is what your inner child has been taught. But remember, this is a learned behavior, and what you learned you can unlearn. It will take a conscious effort, but if you work with your inner child by self-parenting him or her to view the world differently, you will see fantastic results in all areas of your life!

Learning to see bad things as temporary, and teaching your inner child that you are not a victim of life will help you understand that you can dream any life you want and make it a reality!

Let the Healing Begin

Self-Parenting Affirmations

I change my beliefs and I change my life.

If I can't, I must; if I must, I can.

I create my own reality and am responsible for what I create.

Self-Soothing Exercises that Repair and Restore: Learning to Allow Change to Take Place

Change asks us to trust that as we seek, so we will find and recognize what we need. We simply need to allow the process of change to begin and let ourselves to be guided by our inner child. Now you will create a dialogue with your inner child to help you with the change process. Have your journal ready to record your responses to this meditation.

- Focus your eyes on a point near you. Breathe deeply.

- Now invite your inner child into your consciousness.

- Ask your inner child what you need to change to make your life better.

- Ask him or her what you need to do to create a new life for both of you.

- Write down what your inner child tells you to change.

- Ask her/him how to make this change safely, and journal the answer.

- Ask him/her what you need to do to take care of yourself as you make this change, and journal the answer.

Now read over your notes from this meditation. See how your responses resonate with your intuition. Do you feel the wisdom of this new change process? Become willing to implement these changes in beliefs and behaviors.

Change sometimes involves the unexpected, and sometimes not. Change is part of our lives. We can learn to allow ourselves to greet it, to know it, and love ourselves through it.

Codependency Connection

To create positive change, we must change the beliefs that stop us from moving forward. We need to move toward a positive outlook on life. Our learned behavior has kept us in a negative state of mind. Remember that codependents are often taught learned helplessness in their family system. It is part of our codependent experience to learn to expect negative outcomes. We need to counter this learned behavior with positive thinking. To reverse our codependency, we must move in a new direction.

As part of your healing process, make a list in your journal of your relationships that are based in a shared traumatic experience. Next to each name, list the positive and negative aspects of the relationships with each of these people. When your list is complete, think about each relationship carefully and then decide which of these relationships you want to keep and which you should let go.

My Journal

We need to track our belief systems. What we believe is what we live. If we expect negative outcomes, we will receive negative outcomes. If we want to change our lives, we need to change our beliefs.

In your journal, make a list of all the disempowering beliefs you were taught. Leave a few lines between each one. Now develop and write a counterbelief for each one that gives you back your personal power. For instance, if you were taught that poor people stay poor regardless of personal effort, then create a belief that says, "I achieve endless abundance through my belief in hard work and perseverance, and the fact that the universe rewards those of us that believe it will." Another empowering belief could be, "I have all that I need to live an amazing life full of abundance and joy."

Make a separate list of all the beliefs that came from your parents. Are they empowering or disempowering? Make another list of the beliefs that you don't want to keep. Now make a third list, this one of empowering beliefs that you want to replace those old, negative beliefs. As you put together new beliefs, you chart a new path to success.

CHAPTER 15

❧

STEP NINE:

We Learned to Make Amends to Those We Hurt

What lies behind us and lies before us are tiny matters compared to what lies within us.

—OLIVER WENDELL HOLMES

*M*elinda could not believe her therapist was suggesting that she start making amends to the people she had hurt throughout her life. "I don't get it! I am the one that was abused, I am the one that took care of my family when I was a child, and now I am supposed to apologize to everyone I hurt? When do I get my apology? When do people take responsibility for what was done to me? How do I end up making amends before amends are made to me? How does that work?"

Melinda was dumbfounded by her situation. While she knew that she had to take responsibility for what she had done to others, it didn't seem fair. As she developed her list of people to whom she needed to

189

make amends, she started to feel a sense of freedom from the past.
Until she began the process of making amends, she hadn't realized how
much those past hurts had weighed her down.

Making Amends to Those We've Hurt

We all have defects of character, but we came by them honestly.
The coping mechanisms that we developed to deal with our trauma
sometimes hurt other people. Out of our hurt came our lack of
trust, defensiveness, projection, anger, and other hurtful behaviors.
All too often, because of our triggers, our friends, lovers, family,
and coworkers have been victims of our trauma and codependency
reactions.

The first step to establishing healthy relationships with everyone
is to repair the damage we have done to current and past relationships. We are not the only ones who have been hurt. We have also
done our share of hurting others as well. Maybe most of the harm we
caused was unintentional, but harm is harm, and if we are to heal, we
need to take responsibility for what we have done to others.

Trauma Triggers Revisited

As we discussed in earlier chapters, a trauma trigger is an experience that activates a traumatic memory. Triggers can be anything: a
tone of voice, smells, time of day—anything. When we are triggered,
we respond as though we are experiencing our trauma again. Old
memories and fears come up, and we react. We can have very exaggerated responses, striking out at people who have done nothing to
us. Sometimes, we ruin relationships and punish our friends and
lovers for past hurts committed by others.

A trigger experience can be as simple as your friend raising her voice to you in a particular tone that reminds you of the past. Under a circumstance such as this you might become aggressive, thinking that you are protecting yourself, or you might simply refuse to have anything to do with your friend. She, of course, has no idea why you are acting that way, and she feels hurt.

Codependency Reactions

Another block to healthy relationships is directly related to growing up in a dysfunctional home. A home full of chaos and uncertainty leads to learned behavior that is counter to creating healthy intimate relationships. These behaviors were brought into our adult relationships and continued the family tradition of secrecy, control, and self-protection that were the hallmark of our childhoods.

These codependent behaviors must be identified and dealt with if we are going to create healthy intimate relationships. One such aspect of codependency is overfunctioning, taking on more and more responsibility for the relationship so our partner doesn't have to carry any of it. As we overfunction, we become more distant from actual intimacy with our partner.

This overfunctioning is often a part of compulsive self-reliance, a pattern of self-care that we learned in childhood. Compulsive self-reliance often looks like self-sacrifice because we make ourselves so available to help others. We also are usually very competent as we take on responsibility for others. But in reality, all we accomplish through our caretaking is keeping people distant and making it impossible for anyone to help us or take care of us in any way.

Compulsive self-reliance and codependency are not easy to treat. They are behaviors that we learned as part of our survival. And things that are part of our survival, regardless of how problematic, are hard to let go.

If We Abused Anyone

Unfortunately, abused people tend to abuse other people. The literature points to the fact that one outcome of being sexually abused or being hit as a child is the tendency to abuse others. If you have become an abuser in any way, you need help.

Obviously, the first step is to admit what you have done and seek help. You cannot become healthy keeping a secret of this magnitude. And if you do not seek help, your compulsion will continue. Remember, if you have been abused then you have been conditioned to abuse others. This is not an excuse, but it should allow for more compassion for yourself as you deal with this most difficult problem. You will not be able to seek true intimacy with anyone else until you stop abusing others and deal with your underlying issues.

Self-Parenting for Healing

Our inner child has been taught to live in a world that is dark and hurtful. This belief is a function of our upbringing. It is not a fact! The world is the way we see it. There have been hundreds of books written on the power of the mind and its impact on every area of our lives from relationships to money. Controlling our thoughts is critical here. If we can see ourselves in a happy relationship, then we can manifest one. But we still must be willing to do the necessary work. We must work to reeducate our inner child to a better point of view. We must admit our destructive behaviors, become willing to change, and then change.

Let the Healing Begin

Self-Parenting Affirmations

I forgive myself and I forgive others for any harm done.

I am a loving person whose only intention is love.

I am forgiven by God before I ask.

I can choose healthy people to be in my life.

Self-Soothing Exercises that Repair and Restore: We Learn to Forgive Ourselves

Forgiving others is only part of the journey. Ultimately, the most important person to forgive is yourself! The most important person to make amends to is your inner child. When you claim the promise of self-forgiveness, you reveal your love for your inner child and free him or her from a history of pain and trauma. Forgiving yourself is the key to ultimate recovery and to repairing your life.

Have your journal handy to write down your thoughts and feelings after this meditation:

- Soften your focus by looking at a nearby object. Let your conscious mind drift.

- See your inner child. Let her come close.

- See and feel how much she needs love and acceptance.

- Hold her tight. Let her know that you forgive her and she did nothing wrong. Let her know that your love is unconditional and that you are sorry for abandoning her.

- Spend time in this process. Take as much time as she needs; she deserves that.

- When you have finished talking to your inner child, write down what you have experienced.

- List the areas where you have already made amends to your inner child.

- List the areas that still remain where you will need to make amends to yourself.

Now make a list of others you have hurt and invite them into this meditation. You will need to make amends to others in the future, and you need to be careful to do so using discretion. Remember, when you make amends you do so only when it will not hurt yourself or others. But for now, in each case, make spiritual amends in preparation for the time when you will do so in person.

Codependency Connection

Our hurtful behavior is tied to our childhood. Most of the time, we react negatively to a situation because it reminds us of the past. This reaction is an unconscious response to a situation and not intentional. We need to identify these behaviors in order to stop repeating them. We recognize them for what they are: old habits. Old habits die hard, so we must be vigilant as we proceed to deal with them. Try to identify, in writing, your old habits rooted in the past.

My Journal

To complete our recovery plan, we must be willing to make amends to all those we have harmed. We start by making a list of those we harmed and how we harmed them. If possible, we try to identify what defense mechanism was responsible for the harm, and we clearly make a decision to change that behavior in the future. As we identify our triggers and co-dependency traits, we develop a written plan to deal with them as they come up.

In your journal, make a list of your codependent behaviors (refer to the list in Chapter 3 for some common ones). Examine those behaviors from the point of view of how they affect your ability to have an intimate relationship. Next to each symptom that you have listed, write about how it interferes with you and your relationships.

Next, make a list of your triggers and the people who have been affected by them. Now make a decision to apologize to each of them, and explain why you behaved the way you did. It is often helpful to write the apology first, and you can do that next to each name on your list.

CHAPTER 16

❧

STEP TEN:
We Learned to Live in the Present Moment

Humor is a prelude to faith and laughter
is the beginning to prayer.

—REINHOLD NIEBUHR

*A*lex felt free. He was no longer stuck in the past remembering all the negative things that happened or in the future projecting a negative outcome. He had started the meditation class at his therapist's suggestion, and it worked! He was learning to live in the moment.

He was also learning how much of what he thought was going on in his life was a mere projection of his thoughts, not reality. He had thought, for instance, that a particular coworker really disliked him. But when he checked out his perceptions, he found that the coworker was shy and appeared surly as a self-protective mechanism; once befriended, the coworker was quite likeable!

*Alex had come to learn that you cannot do anything about the past,
and the future hasn't happened, so the present is the only real issue at
hand. His level of anxiety dropped as he learned to let go and live one
day at a time.*

The most important thing for trauma survivors and codependents to learn is how to live in the present and how to leave the past behind. Too often we let our trauma and history define who we are for the rest of our lives. And if that definition portrays you as damaged goods or as a flawed individual who is dysfunctional, then you have let the past event shape your life.

We continue the pain of the past when we dwell on the past. Trauma resolution means moving beyond the past. It is a trick of the mind that we relive our traumas over and over. There are current treatments for trauma that help the mind correct this time problem, treatments that help us put in the past what belongs in the past. Please see the Appendix at the end of this book for more information.

Time

For most of our lives, time has been our enemy. What happened in the past continues to haunt us in the present and we fear it will also control our future. We never really feel safe, and we never really know when we will be blindsided by the past. To make matters worse, as part of our trauma, we unconsciously bring people into our present life who are reminiscent of those who abused us. They may be violent, drug-addicted, or narcissistic. In this way, we re-create the past in the present, continuing our nightmare.

We can only be truly safe when we put the past to bed and stop re-creating our trauma and codependent relationships. We must become acutely aware of the signals that our past is introducing itself into our present, and stop the process by becoming acutely aware of our triggers, responding to them in a positive manner, and not giving ourselves over to them.

Inner-Child Dialogue

One way to accomplish this is to have a dialogue with your inner child when you feel triggered. Being triggered means something is sending you danger messages and activating your flight-or-fight responses. This is instinctual and emotional; it is not an intellectual response. You must bring your intellect to the situation and practice slowing down your reaction to the danger stimulus. You need to rationally examine the situation while reassuring your inner child that all is well and that your adult is handling the situation.

All too often, we merge with the feeling when we are triggered and we do not rationally question the reality of the situation; we merge with our fear rather than challenge it. Creating a dialogue with your inner child will allow you to take charge and reassure your inner child that you are capable of keeping you both safe. Having a relationship with your inner child allows for a full integration of your personality, creating a more holistic way of being. It develops inner security and a sense of safety for your inner child.

Take a Daily Inventory

Fundamental to living in the present is the need to take a daily inventory, an examination of your thoughts, actions, and interactions with others. This allows you to take responsibility for them. You want to examine those situations that undermine you or feel uncomfortable. You also want to examine if you have been defensive or aggressive because you have projected your fears on others. You need to take full responsibility for your behavior.

You also want to acknowledge the growth you have exhibited on any given day. You especially want to acknowledge situations that have triggered you, and you want to support your ability to turn the situation around through inner dialogue. As you search out your flaws and correct them, you build a new person who is full of self-confidence and lives with a sense of being in control of his or her life.

Self-Parenting for Healing

Your goal is to be healthy and productive, regardless of your history. Your ultimate goal is to live your life instead of your story. The past is the past; it is not relevant to the present. When we live in the past, we cannot heal because we cannot change the past. What we can do is change the way we relate to the past!

Self-parenting means finding ways to keep yourself in the present, because living in the present moment is the secret to a happy life. The past is gone forever; the future is not here; we only have the present.

Let the Healing Begin

Self-Parenting Affirmations

At last, at last, the past is past;
I've broken through and won.

The past does not equal the future.

I create my own reality and am
responsible for what I create.

I know that my triggers are windows into
the part of me that I need to heal.

Self-Soothing Exercises that Repair and Restore: Learn Thought Replacement

One technique for self-soothing is to stop a thought in its tracks and substitute another in its place. This process—called "stop-think"—which is used in schools, abstinence programs, therapeutic settings, and other settings—is a way to control habitual thinking that may be counterproductive. This technique allows us to stop mind-racing—the constant replay of traumatic events in our heads—which is a major energy drain for trauma survivors and codependents. The ongoing attempt to control the past, the present, and the future is something at which we simply cannot succeed.

Negative thoughts have no value but to undermine us. And who needs to be undermined, especially by themselves? Negative thoughts will retraumatize us if we let them. Bad thoughts are bad habits. But bad habits can be broken, and one of the most successful ways to do so is to challenge those negative thoughts consistently.

Using the "stop-think" process will enable you take charge of your thoughts and not let them take charge of you. It is important to remember that we are not our thoughts, and we are not our feelings. We do not have to dwell on negative thoughts or give over to bad, fearful feelings. We can decide what we think and what we feel. And if we do not like a feeling state we are in—fear, for example—we can change it immediately.

Use your journal to help you identify your negative thoughts and break the pattern by using the "stop-think" approach:

- Make a list of habitual, intrusive thoughts that haunt you.

- Now make a list of positive replacement thoughts that would reverse the effect of the negative thoughts.

- Make a commitment that every time you have a negative, intrusive thought you will implement the "stop-think" process of thought replacement. Put your commitment in writing by composing a positive statement in your journal.

Every time you have a negative thought, visualize your list of positive replacement thoughts and focus on them. Do this until it becomes a new habit!

 ## Codependency Connection

We have control only in the present. We cannot change the past or control the future. Codependency is learned behavior from the past. We apply coping strategies in the present that came from situations in the past that are no longer present. When we live in the present moment, we allow ourselves to drop our codependent behaviors and leave them where they belong—in the past.

We are healthy when we can live in the present. We will be tempted to allow past traumas to define our present circumstance. We need to be fully aware to keep our consciousness in the present moment. Try to identify in writing the ways you avoid being in the present. This can come in the form of focusing on regrets from the past or worrying about the future. Remember the only time that is important is right *now!*

 ## My Journal

Perhaps one of the most important things you can do for your recovery is to learn to live in the present and leave your trauma and codependency behind. A daily inventory will keep you on track and in the present. It is important to learn new behaviors and practice them to counteract bad habits that

were conceived out of your trauma. As you chart your recovery, allow for a daily review of your thinking and behavior.
Be sure to examine your daily behavior for signs of old
codependent behaviors and/or trauma triggers.

One way of staying in the day is to develop a daily inventory that examines your thoughts and behaviors for the day.
The following is a list of questions to ask yourself and journal
about:

- Are my thoughts negative or positive?

- Are my interactions with others based in fears
  and triggers?

- Are my behaviors grounded in present or past
  thinking?

- Have I used my inner-child dialogue to challenge
  my fears?

- Have I used Stop-Think to deal with oppressive
  thinking?

- Have I injured anyone?

- Have I expressed gratitude for the blessings I have?

CHAPTER 17

∾

STEP ELEVEN:
We Sought Through Prayer and Meditation to Improve Our Relationship with God

*I do not know whether I was then a
man dreaming I was a butterfly
Or whether I am now a butterfly
dreaming I am a man.*

—CHUANG-TZU, CHINESE PHILOSOPHER, 396–289 BCE

M*ary is a Native-American woman who has been diagnosed with
complex trauma. As a child, she witnessed her cousin's suicide;
from the age of twelve, she was sexually abused by a neighbor; and
her former boyfriend was physically abusive to her. Mary has been*

to counselors many times, but she feels little relief from her trauma symptoms or her inability to sleep, her nightmares, and her migraines.

It wasn't until her elder spoke to her about healing that she really started to leave her past behind. Her elder told her that all her trauma had happened to her "earth suit," not to her. Her elder said nothing could really hurt her true self, because that self was inside her earth suit and untouchable. When Mary heard that, she suddenly felt relief. She realized that the real part of her had not been raped or beaten; she was intact and not damaged goods. She finally realized that she had an inner world that was inviolate. Mary began to understand that her spiritual self can be hurt but is always intact.

Mary decided to get more familiar with this inner self inside her earth suit. She started to attend prayer ceremonies and go to sweat lodges. She learned how to meditate and get in touch with her spiritual self and Mother Earth. She began to feel wonder at the newfound insights she was experiencing as a result of her spiritual practice. She found peace in her stillness for the first time.

Peace of mind is not easy to attain for codependents or trauma survivors. It is hard for traumatized individuals to learn how to be still and pray or meditate. And most codependents who have been traumatized are outer directed. They are hypervigilant individuals who are constantly scanning their environment for clues. They spend all their time in the outer world trying to maintain some sense of security and safety. They don't develop a connection to their inner world. When you spend a lifetime looking over your shoulder it is hard to let go and give over to quiet and peace.

True safety comes from an understanding that genuine security comes from inside. The outside world can never really make you feel secure; real security comes from a connection to a higher power. Real security comes from being based in a state of inner peace and clear connection to the spiritual side of your being, the part of yourself that is connected to the universal oneness. When you pray and meditate, you strengthen that connection to something greater than yourself.

Thought Is Prayer

Prayer is different from meditation. Prayer is an offering up. Prayer is manifesting through thought, while meditation is paying attention to the silence and an absence of thought. It is important to remember that thought is prayer and all prayers are answered. What we think becomes manifest, so it is important to control thought, especially negative thought! Prayer is conscious contact with the infinite intelligence within you, and that intelligence always responds in the affirmative.

Everything that comes out of your mouth is a form of prayer. What you say creates your reality. If you say "I am poor," you're claiming poverty as your reality. Because speech and thoughts are prayers and the universe answers all our prayers, when we say we are poor we are manifesting poverty. If we say we are sick, we will manifest illness.

We need to listen to ourselves and only speak of ourselves in a positive way. Many trauma survivors and codependents talk of themselves in negative ways. They say things like "I am damaged because I have been raped," or "I am the child of an alcoholic, and that has ruined my capacity to have a successful relationship." Those comments and comments like them are not true. But when we state them as though they are fact, we give an order to the universe to manifest them. We need to ask the universe for good things if we want good things in our life. The universe receives our thoughts—especially when our emotions are tied to our thoughts—as a demand.

Because we are children of pain and disappointment, we often become pessimistic about life, and we expect little. We get what we expect, so our expectations therefore must be positive! It is important for us to believe that our birthright is joy and abundance. We need to proclaim what is right with us and recognize and expect the best for ourselves.

We need to see our trauma as a situation that happened but does not define us in any way. We need to learn to proclaim the best for ourselves and to only talk of ourselves in a loving, positive manner. Pray abundance and love into being by proclaiming them as true.

Every thought and feeling is your prayer. Our minds are the projectors, we are the projectionists. Make the movie of your life a love story, not a horror movie.

Meditation

The point of meditation is to still the mind. Meditation is a conscious stilling of self. It is the launching pad for transcending our ego and communicating with God.

All the great religions have a version of meditation that is practiced as a means to move beyond the ego and listen to spirit. The divine source is just a thought away. To meditate, we must quiet the mind. To quiet the mind, we must change our old behavior. We must move from being compulsively busy to becoming still and quiet.

When we meditate regularly, we move beyond our ego to a deeper sense of self—a self that is connected to the universal self. Once we make that connection, we can experience the "peace beyond understanding" that the mystics refer to: a peace that is inviolate, eternal, and always available. When that happens, we come in contact with our true and eternal self.

There many ways to meditate. The path of meditation you take isn't important, as long as you pick one and stay with it. Zen, insight, transcendental, and mindful meditations are just a few. Once you focus on one practice, you will find that the fruits of your work will become increasingly manifest.

One particular practice we recommend is centering prayer, created by Basil Pennington, a Trappist monk. Centering prayer is a modern practice based on the early Christian mystical traditions. It is very simple. You find a quiet place, take deep breaths, and relax. You put yourself in a meditative state by quietly chanting a word or phase that centers you. Some people just say God or Jesus or Abba (which means "father") or Mother Earth over and over again to bring them to a sacred space. Once you are quiet, you allow your thoughts to flow past you like dandelions in the wind, without attaching to them any thought in particular.

Meditation allows us to enter into a state where we feel our love for God, and we feel God's love for us. We continue our simple mantra until we wish to return to consciousness. Doing this practice daily allows us to "wear the world as a loose garment." Meditation brings us closer to our real self, the spiritual core that is always with us even when we ignore it.

Self-Parenting for Healing

Once we enter this world of quiet, peaceful, loving wonder, the circumstances of our life fail to have much meaning to us. We are no longer defined by our circumstances. We have a greater reality that is the true definition of who we are. This is self-parenting at its highest. When we access our universal consciousness to become part of the self-parenting process, we move into a brand-new world of love, self-acceptance, and abundance.

Let the Healing Begin

Self-Parenting Affirmations

I am a spiritual being having a human experience.

I am connected at all times to my spiritual self.

I believe in a benevolent universe that
is always sending me love.

I tap my inner joy and love it.

I tap my inner joy on a daily basis.

 ## Self-Soothing Exercises that Repair and Restore: Learn to Become Quiet

Meditation. Many of us are confused about meditation, which is the art of developing spiritual listening skills. Spiritual listening skills are underdeveloped in western society, but they are easy to develop. Meditation can be chanting or visualization or simply looking at a flower or just watching the rain. Try this exercise:

- Let your breath move naturally and watch it. Do not force anything.

- Become immersed in your inner self. Turn your mind and senses inside. If thoughts arise, simply let them come and go.
- Meditate with the awareness that you are a witness of the mind.

The moment your thoughts become still, the light of the creator will shine through. When your meditation is complete, write down your experience.

Remember that like anything else, meditation will yield results only to the degree it is done on a regular basis. Meditation is exercise, and like any exercise, it gets better with practice.

Prayer. Prayer is different from meditation. Prayer is asking God for help. It is the raising of our consciousness toward the universal source. Prayer is difficult for many people because it has become very formalized. The most effective prayer is one from the heart, so begin with this exercise:

- Let us prepare to pray from our hearts.
- Let us prepare to pray as a child would.
- Breathe deeply and let yourself relax. Focus your eyes on a nearby object and let your consciousness drift.
- See your inner child coming toward you.
- Ask your inner child to open his or her channel to God.
- Ask your inner child to help you write a prayer from his or her heart to God.
- Let the prayer emerge from your inner child.

- Write it down in your journal and read the prayer from the heart.

There are many ways to meditate and pray; these are just two. Whatever you choose will work as long as you practice! For the "Indian Prayer for Peace", visit www.ogormandiaz.com.

Codependency Connection

Codependency is about seeking outside approval. Independence is about seeking your own approval. When we practice prayer and meditation, we learn how to be inner-directed. We learn how to find our own guidance through our own intuition. We become self-sufficient in our own spiritual practice. We are no longer guided by what others tell us but what our inner spirit says we should do. We have always been informed by our intuition, but often we didn't listen to it. Think back to good and bad decisions you made and whether or not you were guided. Write down your experiences with your intuition.

My Journal

Develop a plan for making time to meditate and pray. Make your inner development a priority by setting a specific time every day for meditation, spiritual readings, and prayer. Write down your experiences in your journal; validate them for the wisdom and guidance they contain. Meditation and prayer can serve as the beacon light that will guide you on your journey to health and wholeness.

CHAPTER 18

∾

STEP TWELVE:

We Learned to Give Meaning to Our Suffering and Live as Examples of Love and Service to Others

We who lived in concentration camps can remember the men who walked through the huts comforting others, giving away their last piece of bread. They may have been few in number, but they offer sufficient proof that everything can be taken from a man but one thing: the last of the human freedoms—to choose one's attitude in any given set of circumstances, to choose one's way.

—VIKTOR FRANKL, M.D., CONCENTRATION CAMP
SURVIVOR AND FOUNDER OF LOGOTHERAPY

For the first time in her life, Jodi wasn't taking care of anyone. She had finally left her husband after years of putting up with his drinking and affairs. With the help of her therapist, Jodi had finally set limits and boundaries for her extremely needy and intrusive family. She had changed jobs and was finally in a job where she was a valued team member. Her life seemed to be in order for the first time, but she felt empty. She knew that part of that emptiness came from the loss of all the craziness in her life. But the chaos had filled a vacuum, and when she moved away from the people who caused the chaos in her life, she felt lost. This new space was unfamiliar, and in a weird way, it was boring.

Now, with a new life beginning, she felt directionless, like a boat without a rudder. And though she was scared, she was excited as well. For the first time in her life, she was living her life just for herself, and she was excited by the possibilities.

Jodi started thinking of all the things she hadn't done that she could do now. For most of her life, her mission had been to take care of the people around her. For most of her life, her rape had defined her; it had become her story, the only story she knew.

Now, Jodi was finally experiencing the reality of being free, of being someone other than the victim she had always been or the caretaker she had become. She was simply Jodi: a good woman who had been a good child and a great mate, and who was now getting ready to make her mark on the world, to do what she could to alleviate pain in others, share her love, and contribute all of her gifts to the world.

Jodi finally realized how the dysfunction in her life had served her. She saw how it had kept her occupied so she didn't have to deal with her own feelings and really focus on what gave meaning to her life.

It's not the things we have that end up defining us; it's the people we love and the causes we serve that define us. For many of us, having terrible experiences can define our lives if they give us purpose and do not overwhelm us. We who have suffered because of life circumstances—whether because of terrible things that happened to us or things that we witnessed—are in fact heroic! Surely we do not need to suffer to find meaning in our lives. But if we suffer as many of us have, our ability to rise above our pain, to give meaning to suffering and to find hope through despair, strengthens us as a people.

Why have we suffered? What meaning is there in being raped or beaten, being in a war, or witnessing a death? Why do we suffer? Is life just meaningless happenstance?

Life Is All About Choice

Viktor Frankl, M.D., who we discussed in Chapter 4, said: "Everything can be taken from a man but . . . the last of the human freedoms —to choose one's attitude in any given set of circumstances, to choose one's way." He wrote this observation based on his experiences in a concentration camp. But many of us have lived with our own horror: the trauma of rape, war, and violence; or the pain of growing up in an alcoholic home. Many of us have lived in our own form of a concentration camp. We have watched people overcome unspeakable horror with dignity and courage; they are role models for us. They, like we, have survived. People who face life-threatening illness with resolve and a will to live fully to the end of their lives are role models, too. We cannot control what life gives us as challenges; all we can control is how we behave when those challenges face us.

The late actor Christopher Reeve, who portrayed Superman on screen and later became a quadriplegic, said in his autobiography,

Still Me, "I think a hero is an ordinary individual who finds strength to persevere and endure in spite of overwhelming obstacles." That statement certainly defines all of us who have thrived in spite of our negative life experiences. We are all heroes!

Logotherapy, a therapy form created by Viktor Frankl, sees the very essence of human existence in responsibleness. Love and responsibleness define us as human beings. When we choose to thrive in the face of pain and move beyond our stories to create new ones with happy endings, we take control and are no longer victims. We who have faced much know the worst that life can offer. There is truly no situation that can overwhelm us, if we fight and don't let it define us. We are not trauma victims; we are people who are much more than the trauma we faced. In some cases, due to the trauma we faced, we are better people.

From great suffering comes great compassion or great cruelty. It is up to you to decide how your life will unwind and what you will leave as a legacy.

Life Is All About Love

Dr. Frankl wrote that three things give meaning to life: the gifts of our work that we share with the world, loving another authentically, and the stance we take toward unavoidable suffering.

Unconditional love gives our lives meaning, regardless of the plight we find ourselves in. In his book *The Will to Meaning,* Dr. Frankel writes that it was the thought of his wife that kept him alive while he was in the concentration camps. His vision of those he loved was enough to overcome the suffering of the camps.

Many of us have forgotten how to love. In our rush for sensation and acquisition, we forget that other people are what life is all about, and that love is the key to a meaningful life. No one can become fully aware of the very essence of another human being unless he loves that other person. In the end, we are solitary beings seeking out each other to bridge our lives. The only way to break from our isolation is to love and connect with one another.

Those with codependence who have been traumatized are people who are full of love. But we are frightened to trust another enough to love because in many cases, those we have loved have betrayed us. But the only way to have a full life is to love fully, to give yourself totally to another, and to move beyond fear. In this way, we imbue our lives with meaning.

It is not the trauma and pain in our life that define us, but the manner in which we face that pain. For many of us who have suffered trauma or who grew up in alcoholic homes, the very suffering we experienced has made us finer people. We have faced inevitable pain with honor and bravery and have managed to avoid being defined by that experience.

Bear witness to the uniquely human potential at its best and, transform a personal tragedy into a triumph; turn your predicament into a human achievement!

Perhaps the best prescription for a meaningful life can be found in St. Francis of Assisi's Prayer for Peace:

Lord, make me an instrument of your peace.
Where there is hatred, let me sow love;
where there is injury, pardon;
where there is doubt, faith;
where there is despair, hope;
where there is darkness, light;
and where there is sadness, joy.

In the end, the best life is one of service. Service is love in action. When we live a life of service, we live a life of love. We might think that up to now we have lived a life of service because we took care of so many people, especially our families. Many of us with codependence who are trauma survivors have also picked careers that are in the helping fields. But sometimes we don't make a *choice* to be of service—we feel *obligated* to be of service, and that's the difference.

Self-Parenting for Healing

In the end, we learn that giving meaning to our pain has been a major part of our healing. When we self-parent and give meaning to our suffering, we empower ourselves to master our past. By making use of our pain to help others, we create healing for ourselves and win against the perpetrators.

Let the Healing Begin

Self-Parenting Affirmations

*I am more than anything I experience because
I am a child of the universe.*

*I am a servant of God's will, and it is
a pleasure to do his will.*

*I am part of the human family, and my
obligation is to all human beings.*

 ## Self-Soothing Exercises that Repair and Restore: Learn Your Purpose

We need to reaffirm our fundamental purpose to be of service to our fellow passengers on Spaceship Earth. Try this simple meditation on service:

- Relax and unfocus your eyes so you can look inward.

- Inhale and exhale slowly and deeply.

- See your inner child; bring him or her close.

- Ask your inner child, "What is my higher purpose?"

- Ask your inner child, "What is my greatest wish?"

- Ask your inner child, "How can I be of service?"

- See yourself perform the tasks that are most meaningful for you each day.

As you proceed each day connected to your core purpose,
you will become more and more satisfied with your life. You
will act from your spiritual core instead of your ego. You will
be in your truth.

The Codependency Connection

There is a great deal of difference between caring about
others and living a life of service and codependency. Codependency is a compulsive act that we have learned to do as a
function of the dysfunction in our family. Service is something
we do willingly with no expectation of reward or recognition.
It is something that is done out of brotherhood and love,
not from fear of retribution. When we leave codependency
behind, we are able to live as free people who can truly give
from their hearts because of love for humanity. When we
leave codependency behind, we find our interdependence
and fellowship with others. We move into true partnership
with everyone as a spiritual being sharing love. Write down
the times you remember being of service and helping others.
Record how you felt when you were giving back. Remember
that compulsive helping is not being of service—it's being a
victim. So also try to distinguish when you were giving freely
and not out of codependency.

My Journal

We are part of something much greater. We are part of our history and we are part of human history. When we see ourselves in a greater context, we are not so apt to take ourselves so seriously but are instead able to see the greater picture. This exercise will allow you to get perspective on your life. As you review each question or prompt, write your thoughts in your journal.

- Review your life from your deathbed. What can you point to that gave it meaning?
- Write an obituary for yourself as though you have already lived a full life.
- List ways that you have been a role model as a:

Spouse or lover	Employee
Friend	Community member
Parent	Spiritual being

Review your lists and see where you need to make more of an effort.

Now make a commitment to make some improvement as a role model each day. Let your focus be on service and love and on the small tasks you can accomplish in one day.

In the end, as we prepare to leave this life, it will be our service to one another that will decide the worth of our days. Our love for each other, our kindness toward one another, and our integrity will stand as a monument to our life's work. We do not want regrets when we reach the end of our time here.

EPILOGUE

Where do we go from here? The first step is to understand what type of trauma you have and its impact on your life physically, mentally, and spiritually. In order to change, we must become very clear about what happened to us and its effect on us. Once we are clear, we can chart a clear road to health and wholeness. Just becoming clear on the types of trauma we experienced allows us to relax, knowing that we can now take steps to remedy our situation.

The same can be said for codependency. We need to examine our childhood and become very clear on the dysfunctional behaviors we learned growing up that are part of the way we function in the world. Some of our coping mechanisms were helpful, but many are also dysfunctional. We examine them and write them down in our recovery plan. Now we have a road map to recovery. We are no longer hiding from the truth. Half the battle is to be clear and understand what it is that needs correcting. Remember that trauma and codependency are complex and subtle, so give yourself permission to take the time necessary to learn and comprehend

You are worth that time, so take it! Make notes in your journal when you identify with something you read. For some of you, concepts like secondary trauma and intergenerational trauma may be entirely new and foreign. You may not have been aware that you were even affected. You now see how families teach dysfunctional belief systems and behaviors to one another and pass it down like an inheritance.

For those of you who have careers where you listen to the trauma of others, it may come as a surprise that you "caught" trauma from your patients, coworkers, and friends. You may not have thought this was possible, but on reflection, you will see that secondary trauma does indeed exist, and it has affected you.

Now that you see how this happens, you can do something about it. You can leave behind those learned behaviors that are working against you and you can embrace those that work for you. But the important thing is that *now you have a choice.*

Whatever you thought you had to do or be before, you now know is simply a choice. And choices can be changed at any time. Change is not easy, especially when we are talking about long-term behaviors that have worked for us in the past. Our psyche sometimes rebels against leaving behind familiar behaviors we don't always want to abandon.

Self-Parenting as a Tool

As we move toward health and change behaviors and belief systems, we will meet with resistance. We need to exert our will when this happens. We need to self-parent. Our inner child is full of fear. Our inner child does not want to be hurt again and will hold on for dear life to toxic behaviors because that is all he or she knows.

That is why the self-soothing techniques we have taught you are so important. You will need to implement them when you feel resistance to change, which is your inner child's way of crying out for help and self-parenting. Through techniques like self-soothing and inner dialogues, and simply learning to apply your intellect to situations in which you are getting emotionally flooded, you utilize tools for change. These tools are yours to use anytime you need them, but they are useless unless you access them.

Change is possible, but we must do the work. Tools left in the toolbox can't build a house. And if we are going to build or rebuild our house, we need a plan.

Charting Your Recovery

As we said in Step One, your chart to recovery is your plan for your new house. It is the way you will change lifelong toxic patterns. Having specific solutions to specific problems makes real change not only possible, but probable. Without a plan, you are flying blind trying to guess your way into recovery. With a specific written plan, you have a road map to your own abundance and joy.

The chart to recovery will highlight the areas that you have the most problems with as well as the areas that need little work. If you work the plan, you will become clear on your strengths as well as your weaknesses and you will find out you have more of the former than the latter.

It is essential that you religiously maintain your chart to recovery. Not only is it a road map, it is a progress report. When we first go to a gym, it is hard to see results, and we often have more pain than gain. In short order we get discouraged, and we stop going to the gym. Don't let that happen with your recovery: use your chart to recovery to stay motivated. You will see the change as you keep a daily inventory.

Progress is measured in many ways. Identifying your issues is progress; identifying how your issues affect you is progress; and implementing strategies to change negative behaviors is progress. If we make a daily inventory of our progress, marking what we want to change and what we want to manifest each day, we will see our progress grow!

Keeping a clear vision in your mind of how you want to be and what you want in your life will become a constant thought. As we said before, thought is prayer made manifest. Over a century ago, James Allen wrote in his groundbreaking essay "As a Man Thinketh" that the thought process has been used to manifest success for tens of thousands of people—and it will work for you. As long as you keep what you want to be and how you want to behave in the forefront of your mind, you will see results.

Let the Healing Begin!

APPENDIX

Resources and Websites:
When Additional Supports Are Needed

Exploring additional ways of healing is a terrific idea, one we eagerly endorse. But a word of guidance is in order as we discuss additional resources to explore. Any work that you do that involves using your body may trigger *body memories,* remembrances that are stored physically. This is normal and nothing to be afraid of. Just be aware of this possibility and plan for how you want to handle the situation if it arises.

You might want to consider informing your massage therapist, physical therapist, or even yoga or t'ai chi teacher that you are a trauma survivor, and that certain postures or gestures may be somewhat loaded for you emotionally. If you are in psychotherapy, you will want your psychotherapist, social worker, or psychologist to be in communication with your massage therapist, acupuncturist, or physical therapist just as you would wish them to be in communication with your physician if you are taking medication. Body memories that come up can be more effectively managed by all of you through communicating and planning for how to identify and soothe these very normal manifestations of trauma.

Consider keeping a journal of how you feel during and after yoga, physical therapy, martial arts, or a massage. Write about the thoughts that come to mind, the feelings, urges, and even smells.

And finally, know that through the utilization of these additional supports, you can facilitate your healing. Some of these supports are:

Yoga. This word stems from *Yu,* which means to integrate or unite. This is exactly what is being done in yoga: you are uniting the unconscious to the universal consciousness and integrating your body, mind, and spirit. The three main yoga structures used to obtain universal harmony are exercise, breathing, and meditation. In yoga, you treat your body with the care and respect it should have as your temple; it is your primary instrument used to achieve and grow in life.

One of the most beneficial parts of yoga in regard to trauma resolution is the deep breathing aspect of it, or meditation. Many people believe that meditation means not thinking about anything and clearing your mind; this is not so. The activities of the mind are brought into focus resulting in a quiet mind that is used to relieve issues and stressors. Yoga is a practice that helps people feel more agile, healthy, and relaxed. If you have experienced trauma, yoga can save your life.

Yoga helps to release the stress and agitation on your mind, helps you pay attention to what is going on in the present, and regulates the nervous system, which in return eases emotions such as fear, loneliness, and helplessness. Trauma and the body are linked; your mind sends messages to your body to convince it that the trauma that caused the fear is still present, which is why you continue to have stress and tension in your muscles.

T'ai chi ch'uan (Tai chi). This is a martial art practice from China that is used for both its defense training and health benefits. T'ai chi is associated with traditional Chinese medicine because its movements are aligned with the body and its healing mechanisms. The slow, incremental movements have been proven to have tremendous health benefits, such as speeding up your metabolism. They work each individual muscle (including your lungs), which helps your physical appearance as well as eases stress. Many researchers have found that t'ai chi practices promote flexibility, control, and cardiovascular health. T'ai chi significantly increases your psychological well-being as well, which includes decreasing anxiety and depression and reducing stressors, especially those associated with trauma.

Martial Arts. This is a series of defense skills and techniques originally used for combat situations. The foundation of martial arts stems back to ancient Asia and fourteenth-century Europe. Different sects of martial arts include karate, judo, taekwondo, and kickboxing. Karate concentrates on striking maneuvers such as punching and kicking, while judo practices pinning and strength techniques. Although most martial arts focus on techniques used in battle situations, they are also beneficial for physical exercise, mental endurance, and spiritual advancements; most important, martial arts will instill discipline in oneself. One must learn to control the mind, especially those in treatment or receiving therapy. Discipline is key to overcoming any obstacle in life. A disciplined mind is a healthy mind.

Massage. This word comes from the French word meaning "to knead," and this type of therapy promotes relaxation of the body by literally rubbing the tension out of layers of muscle and inner tissue. There are several different types of massage therapy, and the art of manipulating the muscles stretches back to 460 BCE in ancient China. Modern massage treatments involve lying on a cushioned table surrounded by the aroma of sensual oils and soothing sounds. Some believe massage treatments can help lower blood pressure and even improve symptoms in some illnesses. Because the muscles are technically being "worked out," the body releases the same endorphins one would experience during physical exercise. An endorphin is a chemical acting as a neurotransmitter that sends a sense of well-being and happiness to the brain, and these feelings are especially beneficial for trauma resolution.

Acupuncture. An alternative medical treatment that uses pin-size needles to prick the skin and find nerve endings. Such treatment is said to cure illnesses, treat wounds, and improve healing overall. Acupuncture treatments date back to 200 BCE in ancient China. Acupuncture is highly individualized, and most practitioners treat each patient differently based on body and mind stressors. Acupuncture is still considered an "alternative" form of treatment, said to be useful but lacking sufficient evidence to be proven effective. Even so, acupuncture therapy is active in trauma recovery as a relaxing and personalized technique.

Chiropractic Treatment. Another form of alternative therapy that strictly focuses on the musculoskeletal system. Chiropractic treatment was founded in the 1890s and is generally practiced in North America and Australia. Many early practitioners, known as "straights," believed that all illness stems from a defect in the spine. This led to the belief that if the spinal alignment could be corrected, so could the ailment. Modern chiropractors, known as "mixers," focus on relaxation with hot and cold stones, massage, and exercise for the bones and muscles in addition to spinal manipulation. Although chiropractic treatments are still considered an alternative therapy solution, chiropractic is the third largest healthcare choice among consumers.

Alcoholics Anonymous (AA)/Narcotics Anonymous (NA). Alcoholics Anonymous is a self-help group of men and women united in a journey to recover from alcoholism. The fellowship originated in 1935 in Akron, Ohio. It is open to people of any race, religion, and gender. In over 150 countries, AA meetings are set up at local facilities and welcome those seeking guidance in their recovery. Meeting goers are asked to share their stories and struggles with alcohol during the meeting. There are several different types of meetings including "Big Book" discussions, open and closed meetings (for everyone and just for alcoholics, respectively), and 12-step meetings that focus on working the twelve steps of recovery. Narcotics Anonymous is a 12-step program that is modeled after AA and is for men and women who have a problem with drugs. The only requirement to be a member is a desire to stop using drugs, to meet regularly, and to help each other in the group stay clean.

Al-Anon/Nar-Anon. Al-Anon is a support group that consists of and for family and friends of alcoholics. This is where loved ones can express their feelings, experiences, and give advice to each other about their interactions with the alcoholic. Membership is open to anyone who has a relative or friend who is an alcoholic. Nar-Anon is a worldwide support group for those who are affected by someone else's drug addiction. Like Al-Anon, it incorporates a 12-step program where people offer advice and their personal experiences in order to share strength and hope with others. The only requirement for membership is to be associated with someone who has an addiction to narcotics.

Psychotherapy. This is a treatment for mental and emotional disorders through the use of psychological techniques. These techniques were developed to help therapists and patients communicate conflicts, share insights into problems, and change behavior, which in return leads to improved social functioning. One of the most significant forms of psychotherapy is *cognitive behavioral therapy*, which can be used in any situation in which there is an unwanted behavior associated with impairment or stress. This form of therapy establishes interventions that are critiqued and designed specifically for people suffering from emotional and psychological difficulties associated with trauma. Adolescents who are suffering severe emotional trauma have responded extremely well to this technique.

Cognitive behavioral therapy helps you evaluate and process your emotions toward traumatic experiences and then helps you manage your emotions in a healthier way. While it doesn't treat physiological effects of the trauma, it is a great way of first measuring your feelings. After that, it can be helpful to use a body-based therapy such as *eye movement desensitization and preprocessing* (EMDR) or *somatic experiencing*. EMDR incorporates cognitive-behavioral therapy with eye movements; this is used to unlock traumatic memories and help resolve them. Somatic experiencing takes advantage of the body's way of healing itself. The major focus is on body sensations about the traumatic experience instead of memories and emotions. From there, somatic experiencing allows you to release the stored up energy through natural forms of release such as crying.

Another new therapy that has been very successful is *rapid trauma resolution* (RTR). It addresses and clears the imprint left by trauma in the areas of the brain that cannot be accessed through "top-down approaches" alone, such as cognitive therapy. Unlike traditional approaches to trauma treatment that require the client to experience painful emotions while reliving the trauma, RTR clears the effects of trauma painlessly. The exact event needing resolution is brought to mind if it has been repressed or forgotten. After creating an experience of positive connection, the therapist helps the client to remain emotionally connected in the present moment while recounting details of the past events. The events are no longer happening, and the client has survived and triumphed over them. The client reprocesses memories of past events, realizes on every level that they are finished and gone, and sheds the painful emotions that have been attached to them. For more information on rapid trauma resolution, please visit www.cleartrauma.com.

Psychotropic medications. Any drug that affects the mind, emotional level, or behavior of someone is considered to be a psychotropic medication. An example of this would be lithium, which is used to treat bipolar disorder, or fluoxetine (Prozac), which is used to treat depression. Thanks to these pharmaceuticals, many people with mental disorders live fulfilling lives; without them those same people might suffer serious and disabling symptoms. But of course, medications work differently for different people—some get great results right away and for others, it takes a little bit longer. While psychotropic medications can be very beneficial, you also have to be aware of some of the possible side effects, which your doctor should explain to you in detail.

One category of medication that is finding increasing use is that of atypical antipsychotics. This is an unfortunate name for a class of medication that is providing significant relief for individuals with more serious trauma such as PTSD. Examples of this type of medication include Abilify and Geodon. Prescribing this class of medication for trauma is considered "off-label," as many have not yet been approved by the FDA for this use. Nevertheless, their use is growing as they help to minimize the mood challenges associated with trauma.

There are other resources available to supplement the ones we have introduced here. The websites listed below contain valuable information and can point you in the right direction.

What is most important is to find a method and resource that feels natural for you and use it! Remember, you are in charge of your recovery. You can live the life you want if you decide you will.

Website Resources

Alcoholics Anonymous
www.aa.org/

Al-Anon Family Group (includes Alateen)
www.alanon.alateen.org

American Red Cross
www.redcross.org/

Faces and Voices of Recovery
www.facesandvoicesofrecovery.org

Join Together
www.jointogether.org

National Child Traumatic Stress Network
www.NCTSN.org

National Association of Children for Alcoholics
www.nacoa.org

National Center on Addiction and
Substance Abuse at Columbia (CASA)
www.casacolumbia.org
www.casalibrary.org (general library)

National Institute on Drug Abuse
www.nida.nih.gov

National Institute on Alcohol Abuse and Alcoholism
www.niaaa.nih.gov

National Clearinghouse on Alcohol and Drug Information
www.health.org

National Organization for Women
www.now.org/

Patricia O'Gorman and Phil Diaz
www.ogormandiaz.com

Patricia O'Gorman, Ph.D.
www.patriciaogorman.com

Rapid Trauma Resolution (RTR) Therapy
www.cleartrauma.com.

Returning Vets and Trauma
www.samhsa.gov/vets/index.aspx
www.ptsd.va.gov/public/web-resources/web-trauma-organizations.asp

Trauma-Related:

Child Trauma Academy
www.childtrauma.org

Trauma Center at Justice Resource Institute
www.traumacenter.org

Trauma Soma
www.traumasoma.com

National Institute for Trauma and Loss in Children
www.starrtraining.org/trauma-and-children

Department of Veteran's Affairs:
National Post Traumatic Stress Network
www.ptsd.va.gov/

National Child Traumatic Stress Network:
Child Trauma Toolkit for Educators
www.nctsnet.org/nctsn_assets/pdfs/Child_Trauma_Toolkit_Final.pdf

Massachusetts Advocates for Children:
Helping Traumatized Children Learn
www.massadvocates.org/download-book.php

Calmer Classrooms: A Guide to Working with Traumatised Children
www.ocsc.vic.gov.au/downloads/calmer_classrooms.pdf

The Heart of Learning: Compassion, Resiliency, and Academic Success
www.k12.wa.us/CompassionateSchools/HeartofLearning.aspx

REFERENCES

Allen, J. 1903; 1948 (DeVorss edition). *As a Man Thinketh.* Camarillo, CA: DeVorss & Company.

American Psychiatric Association (APA). 1994. *Diagnostic and Statistical Manual of Mental Disorders (DSM-IV).* Washington, DC: American Psychiatric Association.

Begley, S. 2007. *Train Your Mind, Change Your Brain.* New York: Random House.

Blackcloud, R. C. 1990. "Warrior who comes home alone." In *A Gathering of Sioux . . . In Honor of Chief Sitting Bull.* Wakpala, SD: Blackcloud Productions.

Carnes, P. 1997. *The Betrayal Bond.* Deerfield Beach, FL: Health Communications, Inc.

Casarjian, R. 1992. *Forgiveness: A Bold Choice for a Peaceful Heart.* New York: Bantam.

Cloitre, M., N. Morin, and O. Linares. 2000. "Children's resilience in the face of trauma." Retrieved September 29, 2011, from the New York University Child Study Center website at http://www.aboutourkids.org/files/articles/jan_feb _0.pdf.

Courtois, C., and J. Ford. 2009. *Treating Complex Stress Disorders: An Evidence-Based Guide.* New York: Guilford Press.

DeGruy, J. "Post-traumatic slave syndrome." Retrieved October 11, 2011, from http://www.joydegruy.com/ptss/index.html.

Encyclopedia of Mental Disorders. "Post-traumatic stress disorder." Retrieved November 10, 2011, from http://www.minddisorders.com/Ob-Ps/Post-traumatic -stress-disorder.html.

Eron, J., and T. Lund. 1996. *Narrative Solutions in Brief Psychotherapy*. New York: Guilford Press.

Evans, K., and J. M. Sullivan. 1995. *Treating Addicted Survivors of Trauma*. New York: Guilford Press.

Fogash, C., and M. Copeley. 2008. *Healing the Heart of Trauma and Dissociation with EMDR and Ego State Therapy*. New York: Springer.

Glass, L. 1995. *Toxic People*. New York: Simon & Schuster.

Frankl, V. 2006. *Man's Search for Meaning*. New York: Beacon Press.

———. 1988. *The Will to Meaning: Foundations and Applications of Logotherapy*. New York: Meridien (Penguin).

Herman, J. L. 1992a. "Complex PTDS: A syndrome in survivors of prolonged and repeated trauma." *Journal of Traumatic Stress* 5: 377–392.

——— 1992b. *Trauma and Recovery*. New York: Basic Books.

Lanius, R., E. Vermetten, and C. Pain. 2010. *The Impact of Early Life Trauma on Health and Disease: The Hidden Epidemic*. Cambridge, England: Cambridge University Press.

Levine, P. 2010. *In an Unspoken Voice: How the Body Releases Trauma and Restores Goodness*. Berkeley, CA: North Atlantic Books.

Liberzon, I., S. Taylor, R. Amdur, T. Jung, K. Chamberlain, S. Minoshima, R. Koeppe, and L. Fig. (1999). "Brain activation in PTSD in response to trauma-related stimuli." *Biological Psychiatry* 45:817–826.

Maté, G. 2003. *When the Body Says No: Understanding the Stress-Disease Connection*. New York: Wiley.

Merton, T. 1971. *Contemplative Prayer*. New York: Doubleday.

Miller, B. A., E. Maguin, and W. R. Downs. 1997. "Alcohol, drugs, and violence in children's lives." In Galanter, M., ed., *Recent Developments in Alcoholism: Volume 13. Alcoholism and Violence*. New York: Plenum Press, 357–385.

National Institute on Alcohol Abuse and Alcoholism (NIAAA). 1989; 2000. "NIAAA Alert: Alcohol and trauma." Retrieved October 6, 2011, from http://alcoholism .about.com/cs/alerts/l/blnaa03.htm.

National Institute on Drug Abuse (NIDA). "Comorbidity: Addiction and Other Mental Illnesses." Research Report Series. Retrieved January 2, 2012 from http://drugabuse.gov/researchreports/comorbidity/diagnosed.html.

O'Gorman, P., and P. Oliver-Diaz. 1990. *Self-Parenting 12 Step Workbook: Windows to Your Inner Child.* Deerfield Beach, FL: Health Communications, Inc.

O'Gorman, P. 1994. *Dancing Backwards in High Heels: How Women Master the Art of Resilience.* Center City, MN: Hazelton Publishing.

Oliver-Diaz, P., and P. O'Gorman. 1988. *12 Steps to Self-Parenting.* Deerfield Beach, FL: Health Communications, Inc.

Osuch, E., and C. Engel. 2004. "Research on the treatment of trauma spectrum responses: the role of the optimal healing environment and neurobiology." *The Journal of Alternative Complementary Medicine* 10(S1): S211–S221.

Pelcovitz, D., B. van der Kolk, S. Roth, F. Mandel, S. Kaplan, and P. Resick. 1997. "Development of a criteria set and a structured interview for the disorders of extreme stress (SIDES)." *Journal of Traumatic Stress* 10: 3–16.

Peterson, C., Maier, S., and Seligman, M. E. P. 1993. *Learned Helplessness: A Theory for the Age of Personal Control.* New York: Oxford University Press.

Reeve, C. 1998. *Still Me.* New York: Random House.

Reyes, G., Ethai, J., Lord, J. 2008. *The Encyclopedia of Psychological Trauma.* New York, NY: Wiley.

Ritskes, R., M. Ritskes-Hoitinga, H. Stodkilde-Jorgensen, K. Baerentsen, and T. Hartman. 2003. "MRI scanning during Zen meditation: The picture of enlightenment." *Constructivism in Human Sciences* 8(1): 85–89.

Ross, G., and P. Levine. "Emotional first aid." Retrieved October 3, 2011, from http://www.ginaross.com/images/emotional_first_aid_brief_guide.pdf.

Roth, S., E. Newman, D. Pelcovitz, B. van der Kolk, and F. S. Mandel. 1997. "Complex PTSD in victims exposed to sexual and physical abuse: Results from the DSM-IV Field Trial for Posttraumatic Stress Disorder." *Journal of Traumatic Stress* 10: 539–556.

Ruiz, M. 1997. *The Four Agreements.* San Rafael, CA: Amber-Allen Publications.

Scaer, R. 2001. *The Body Bears the Burden: Trauma, Dissociation and Disease.* Binghamton, New York: The Haworth Medical Press.

Schechter, D. S., T. Coots, C. H. Zeanah, M. Davies, S. W. Coates, K. A. Trabka, R. D. Marshall, M. R. Liebowitz, and M. M. Myers. 2005. "Maternal mental representations of the child in an inner-city sample: Violence-related post-traumatic stress and reflective functioning." *Attachment and Human Development* 7(3): 313–331.

Schore, A. 1994. *Affect Regulation and the Origin of the Self: The Neurobiology of Emotional Development.* Hillside, NJ: Lawrence Erlbaum Associates.

Siegel, D. 2007. "Mindfulness training and neural integration: Differentiation of distinct streams of awareness and the cultivation of well-being." Retrieved November 17, 2011, from http://scan.oxfordjournals.org/content/2/4/259.fullell-being.

———. 1999. *The Developing Mind: Toward a Neurobiology of Interpersonal Experience.* New York: Guilford Press.

Tedeschi, R., C. Park, and L. Calhoun, Eds. 1998. *Posttraumatic Growth.* Mahwah, NJ: Lawrence Erlbaum Associates.

VA National Center for PTSD. "PTSD and problems with alcohol use: A national center fact sheet." Retrieved October 3, 2011, from: http://www.forests.com/ptsdalch.html.

van der Kolk, B. 2003. "The neurobiology of childhood trauma and abuse." *Child & Adolescent Psychiatric Clinics of North America* 12: 293–317.

Wolin, S. J., and S. Wolin. 1993. *The Resilient Self: How Survivors of Troubled Families Rise Above Adversity.* New York: Villard.

Yehuda, R., S. Halligan, and R. Grossman. 2001. "Childhood trauma and risk for PTSD: Relationship to intergenerational effects of trauma, parental PTSD, and cortisol excretion." *Development and Psychopathology* 13: 733–753.

Yellow Horse Brave Heart, M. 2005. "From intergenerational trauma to intergenerational healing." *Wellbriety* 6(6): 1–8.

Zlotnick, C., A. L. Zakriski, M. T. Shea, E. Costello, A. Begin, T. Pearlstein, and E. Simpson. 1996. "The long-term sequelae of sexual abuse: Support for a complex post-traumatic stress disorder." *Journal of Traumatic Stress* 9: 195–200.

INDEX

ABOUT THE AUTHORS

Patricia O'Gorman, Ph.D., a psychologist in private practice in East Chatham and Albany, New York, is noted for her work in trauma, families, children of alcoholics, child welfare, mental health, and substance abuse. She was one of the first researchers on children of alcoholics in the early 1970s, documenting the impact of alcoholism and sobriety on adolescent development, and went on to create the Department of Prevention and Education for the National Council on Alcoholism and Drug Dependence (NCADD). She has served as an international consultant to organizations in preventive and clinical strategic planning. Dr. O'Gorman is a cofounder of the National Association for Children of Alcoholics, and she has held positions that include clinical director of a child welfare agency, executive director of an agency serving survivors of crime and abuse, and director of prevention for NIAAA. She is a veteran of numerous television appearances, including *Good Morning America, Today,* and *AM Sunday.* She is the author of *Dancing Backwards in High Heels: How Women Master the Art of Resilience,* coauthor (with Phil Diaz) of *The Lowdown on Families Who Get High, 12 Steps to Self-Parenting for Adult Children, 12 Steps to Self-Parenting Workbook,* and *Breaking the Cycle of Addiction,* and coauthor (with Peter Finn) of *Teaching About Alcohol,* as well as numerous articles in magazines including *Addiction Today, Counselor,* and *Recovery.* She brings the same type of seminal thinking to the topic of trauma and codependency that she used to help create the Children of Alcoholics movement.

Phil Diaz, M.S.W., is the director of community development and education for Behavioral Health of the Palm Beaches in Palm Beach, Florida, and has a private practice specializing in the treatment of addiction and trauma at Lifescape Solutions in Delray Beach, Florida. He is the former executive director of the Harrigan Foundation, where he specialized in Gestalt family therapy, and the former CEO of Gateway Community Services, a 300-bed drug treatment facility for adolescents and adults in Jacksonville, Florida, where he pioneered PTSD treatment using EMDR and motivational therapy. He was the founding director of Project Rainbow, the first center for young children of alcoholics, and was the deputy director for substance abuse at the largest community mental health center in New York State, where he pioneered work with the dually diagnosed, drug-addicted person. He is also the former assistant deputy director for prevention in the Office of Demand Reduction with the White House Office of National Drug Control Policy; in this capacity, Diaz was the lead federal official in the development of national and international drug prevention policy.

Diaz is a social worker with more than thirty-five years of experience in the addiction field, child abuse, and trauma. He is also a founding board member of the National Association for Children of Alcoholics, the National Association for Native American Children of Alcoholics, and the founding chairperson of the National Drug Prevention League. His work has appeared in *Women's Day, USA Today,* and Focus on the Family. Diaz is the coauthor of *The Lowdown on Families Who Get High, 12 Steps to Self-Parenting, 12 Steps to Self-Parenting Workbook,* and *Breaking the Cycle of Addiction* as well as numerous articles in magazines, including *Parents, Addiction Today, Counselor,* and *Recovery.* He has received numerous awards for his work including an honorary doctorate in law from Mercy College in New York.